Exam Analysis

J Balogh, PhD

Published by Intelliphonics, LLC
P.O. Box 1438
Menlo Park, CA 94026

ISBN: 978-0-9973617-2-8

Library of Congress Control Number: 2021936148

Printed in the United States of America
First edition

Table of Contents

CHAPTER 1:

Introduction

Who Should Read this Book?

This book is written for any educational professional including professors, instructors, teachers, teaching aides, teaching assistants, graduate students, and volunteers who might need to interpret the results of an exam analysis report. These reports are generated by service companies that automatically score multiple-choice exams.

The statistics you see in these reports are exactly that: statistics. If you are a trained statistician, this book is not for you. But if you are in a field that requires very little statistical analysis, then yes, this book will be essential. Even if you have some formal training in statistics, this book can be helpful. I took many statistics courses as part of my training as an experimental psychologist, but the content that I was taught was customized to my field. For me, the emphasis was on t-tests and ANOVAs, not p-values, point-biserials, and coefficient alpha. I only learned about these concepts later through my experience in the assessment industry. Importantly, most instructors do not have the time or opportunity to launch a side-career in psychometrics, or take a 10-week class in tests and measurements, or even attend an all-day workshop just to interpret the numbers in a few reports. This book is written for professionals who want this knowledge, but who want to get it efficiently. This book allows you to skip all the social niceties and just dive in.

Exam Analysis Tools

There are many exam-analysis tools out there, and this book is not tied to any particular one. There are large overlaps and commonalities between services. Afterall, there are only so many common ways of slicing and dicing test score data.

If there are terms that you are seeing in reports but that do not appear in this book, feel free to get in touch with us and we can help answer your questions: www.intelliphonics.com.

Organization

Most books present each concept one at a time, explain it in detail, give examples, and then at the end, summarize the main points. This book turns this traditional organizational structure on its head. Here you will get what you need quickly and concisely with more detailed information in later chapters.

The rest of this chapter will provide you with a brief overview of the types of reports commonly available and a strategy for how to read them at a high level. Chapter 2 will give you concise explanations of the terms and concepts. This is the meat of the book. An important part of this chapter will be explanations of why this information is relevant and what you can do with it. You have been given a powerful tool in automatic scoring, but if you look at all the interesting information and then just set the report down, all is lost! You should be able to take the information from these reports and apply it. This last point is important; the application of your knowledge about your students' performance on your exams is critical.

The chapter after this (Chapter 3: Implementing the UGIFT Approach) will show you how to make material use of the information in the reports. You will be presented with a comprehensive process on how to take the patterns you are seeing in your reports and use the information to assign grades, customize instruction, and create better exams in the future. Instead of just leaving you with a vague notion that you should increase the reliability of an exam, for example, this chapter will provide concrete advice about how you might go about doing so. By the end, you should have the basic information you need to link the patterns you are seeing in the reports with action.

Finally, the book will explore a few topics in more detail (Chapter 4: Going Deeper). Here you will learn why terms are called what they are, understand the relation between different concepts, and even explore a few equations. The beauty is that you do not have to read these details if you do not have the time or interest. You will have already gotten the essentials and can opt to skip this chapter until the time is right.

Let's begin with an overview of the reports you will encounter along with a high-level framework for analyzing your exams.

Exam Analysis Reports

Most exam-analysis services will generate several reports (since there is too much information to present in just one). Most likely, there will be three reports with the most jargon:

- Summary
- Item Analysis
- Score Distribution

There are other reports of course. Some exam analysis services present individual student reports with learning objectives; others show histograms for the responses for each item. Companies that specialize in exam analysis will always want to offer its customers the most up-to-date and useful information, and will continue to refine report formats and devise new reports in the future. The information presented here is a snapshot of common reports presented by current service companies.

The Summary Report usually presents the class's performance on the exam in aggregate. This report shows such things as the average score, high score, low score, and range. The summary information gives you a feel for how the class performed as a group. The Summary Report might also present reliability numbers. Reliability will be discussed in more detail, but the high-level concept is that reliability describes how consistent and precise the test is. Reliability is important because it is one of three factors that define the quality of a test, the three factors being validity, reliability, and fairness (AERA, APA, NCME, 2014).

The Item Analysis Report dives into the details of each test question. In the testing industry, a question is called an item, which is a term that encompasses all forms of prompts that elicit a response from the student. An Item Analysis Report can tell you which items are performing well and which ones might need to be rewritten for future exams or even removed from the current exam.

The Score Distribution Report gives you more details about how the class performed as a group. Usually, this report will provide you with graphs and numbers that can help with score interpretation and possibly grade assignment.

Steps in Exam Analysis

Exam analysis can be approached from many different angles, and any one method is not necessarily the right or wrong approach. Afterall, instructors are unique people with different personalities, styles, and motives, so it makes sense that one size does not necessary fit all. That said, some might find it useful to have a framework in place to help structure the information from screen after screen of exam-analysis reports. The following approach called UGIFT (Understanding, Grading, Instructing, Future Testing) is a suggested outline for what report to read in what order, including the purpose and potential actionable steps:

UGIFT
Understanding, Grading, Instructing, Future Testing

Understanding the Overall Picture
1. Read the Summary Report
    a. Get an overview of student performance.
    b. Understand the test's reliability.

Grading the Exams
2. Read the Item Analysis Report
    a. Determine if any items need to be eliminated from the exam.
    b. Re-grade if needed.
        (If re-grading, return to Step 1.)
3. Read the Score Distribution Report
    a. Use information to assign grades.

Instructing Based on Performance
4. Reread the Score Distribution Report and Item Analysis Report
    a. Devise a plan for customizing instruction.
    b. Review individual performance.

Future Testing Improvements
5. Reread the Summary Report
    a. Make decisions regarding reliability.
    b. Make decisions about future test difficulty.
6. Reread the Item Analysis Report
    a. Compare item performance with the test blueprint.
    b. Identify items or item types that need future revision.

Of course, this outline is not exhaustive. Reports can provide so much more information, for example, performance of individual students. So, feel free to augment the UGIFT approach to suit your own needs.

Now that you have a basic framework for exam analysis, we can begin looking at the terms and concepts presented in common reports.

Chapter 2:

The Terms and What They Mean

This chapter presents the most common terms in exam analysis reports with explanations of what they mean and how this information is useful to you.

As mentioned in the previous chapter, the three most common reports are the Summary Report, the Item Analysis Report, and the Score Distribution Report.

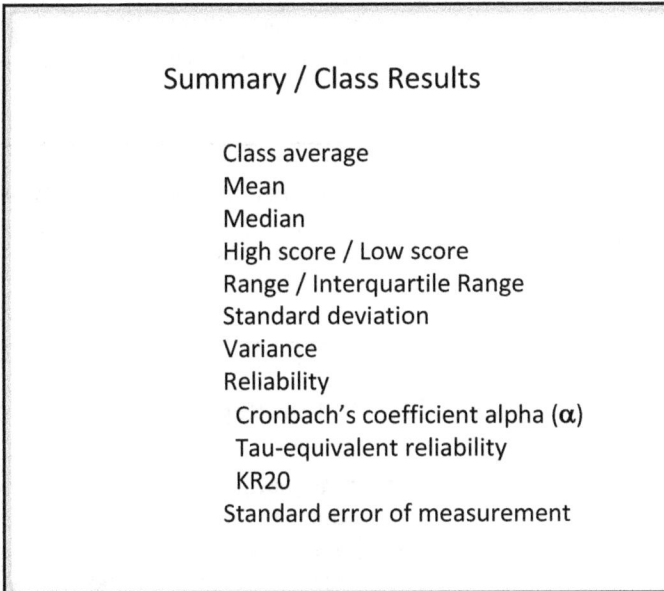

Summary / Class Results

Class average
Mean
Median
High score / Low score
Range / Interquartile Range
Standard deviation
Variance
Reliability
  Cronbach's coefficient alpha (α)
  Tau-equivalent reliability
  KR20
Standard error of measurement

Figure 1. Statistics commonly seen on the Summary Report or Class Results Report.

Item Analysis Report

Class average
Mean
Median
Standard deviation
Variance
% students answer / p-values
Point-biserial / r_{bp}
Reliability without an item
Frequency of each choice
Low performing distractor
Group %s
Lowest 27% and highest 27%
Discrimination Index (D)

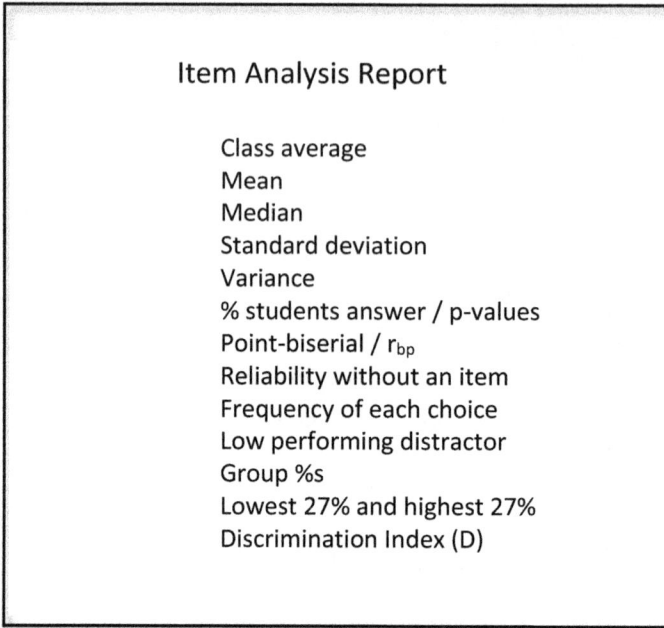

Figure 2. Statistics commonly seen on the Item Analysis Report.

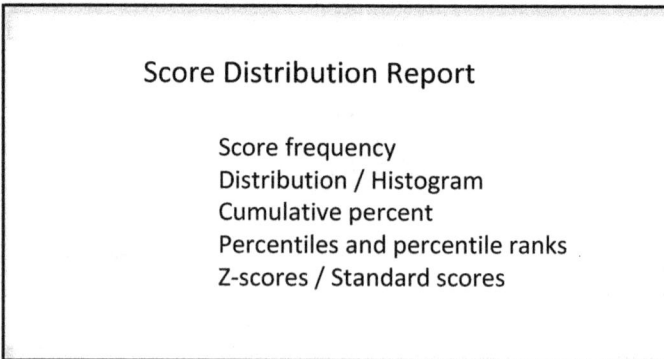

Score Distribution Report

Score frequency
Distribution / Histogram
Cumulative percent
Percentiles and percentile ranks
Z-scores / Standard scores

Figure 3. Statistics commonly seen on the Score Distribution Report.

Not all of the terms listed may appear on your reports. Although there are other reports, the three shown here are usually the ones that include terms requiring the most explanation.

The rest of this chapter is devoted to explaining each term and telling you why it is relevant. Then in Chapter 3, we will spend more time on the step-by-step process of using the information you are reading about here.

The terms will be presented in the order they appear in Figures 1-3.

Let's begin.

Class Average

Pretty much everyone knows what an average is, but it is an important concept. From a group of test scores, it is a way to represent the center.

The technical approach to computing an average is to take the scores for each student's test, add them together, and then divide by the number of students:

Class average =

$$\frac{\text{Aisha's score} + \text{Blake's score} + \text{Connie's score} + \dots}{\text{Total number of students taking the exam}}$$

Why is the class average relevant?

Class Average will tell you if most students aced your test, failed your test, or somewhere in between. This information is useful for monitoring student progress. If the average of the exam is in the middle-to-high range, then most students are understanding the material. Things are on track. If the average is too high, then the test might have been too easy and not able to discriminate those students who are mastering the content from those who are not. If the average is too low then the students did not learn the material, or at least they did not show learning from their performance on the exam.

Knowing where students stand as a group can help you know whether or not you should revisit some of the subject content, change your approach for the next group of students, or adjust the difficulty of future exam questions.

Mean

The mean is the same thing as the average. The exact same thing. If you would like to learn more about why there are two words in the field with the exact same meaning, then see Chapter 4: Going Deeper (page 101).

Median

The median is the middle score. If you were to take all the scores from an exam, rank them from highest to lowest and then find the score in the middle, that score would be the median. For example, if three students took your test and scored 96, 77, and 80, and you ranked these scores from highest to lowest (96, 80, 77), then found the middle score (80), this would be the median.

What if there are four scores and no middle? Let's say the four scores are 96, 90, 80, and 77. Now the median is in between 90 and 80. For cases with an even number of scores, the median is the average of the two middle scores. In this example, the average of 90 and 80 is 85, which is the median. As you can see, the median is not always an observed test score.

Why is the median relevant?

The median tells you what the middle score is, so it is another way of representing the center of a group of scores. If the median is high, then you know that most students did well on the test, and if it is low, you know that there was a big problem with student mastery. It is possible that the students need a review of the material or that students might respond better to a new approach to covering the content in subsequent years, or that the test questions might need to be refined. The median is giving you similar information to the class average.

Why do we care about the median if we already have the average? Even though averages (means) are easy to work with mathematically and therefore get a lot of love in statistics, they have their drawbacks. Sometimes the median is a better way to look at where the center is. One case, in particular, is when there are extreme test scores. Imagine if you had the following five scores: 92, 90, 87, 84, 31. The median would be 87, which is a good representation of where the center of this group is. The mean, however, would be 77. That one extreme score of 31 is dragging down the mean a considerable amount. Because the mean gets pushed around by extreme scores so much, the median is sometimes a better representation of the center.

High Score and Low Score
Range and Interquartile Range

The high score and low score are self-explanatory. When the low score is subtracted from the high score, this gives you the range. The range tells you how much the scores in a group vary. If the scores are similar to one another, the range will be small and if they are wildly different, the range will be large.

The range, by itself, is based on only two scores, which can be misleading if these two scores are not representative of the group. For this reason, some prefer the interquartile range, which is the range of the middle 50% of the scores when the scores are ranked.

Why is the range or interquartile range relevant?

Ranges indicate the degree of variability in the scores. With a small range, you know that students are performing in a similar way, so changes that you make to your exams or instructional approach will most likely impact students in a similar way. With a large range, you have the challenge of addressing varying student needs.

Standard Deviation

The standard deviation gives you information about the spread of the test scores, and does so by incorporating information from each and every score (as opposed to the range which considers only two scores). If scores on a test are widely dispersed across a scale from 0 to 100, then the standard deviation will be large, for example, in the 20s or 30s. If most of the scores are similar to one another, say they are all clustered around 80, then the standard deviation will be very small, for example, 5.

The standard deviation is basically telling you what its name implies: how much the scores standardly deviate from the mean.

Why is the standard deviation relevant?

The standard deviation can give you a sense for how students' scores are spread across the group distribution. If student scores are tightly clustered, then you can target your teaching for the average student in the class and you will reach most of them. If the standard deviation is large, then you know that you have to make accommodations for a considerable range of student abilities. Standard deviation gives you this information at a glance.

Variance

Variance is the standard deviation squared. That's it. That's all it is.

Why is the variance relevant?

Variance gives you similar information to standard deviation because the two are mathematically related. The variance tells you how widespread the scores are as well. If the variance is small, then student scores are clustered together; if the variance is large, then the scores are spread out, suggesting that there are stark differences across student mastery of content.

Frankly, variance is harder to interpret than standard deviation because the variance is based on squared numbers. So unlike, the standard deviation, which is in reference to the total number of points possible on the test, the variance is one step removed from the scale of the exam. Reports might provide you with the variance statistic for completeness, but standard deviation tends to be easier to interpret.

Reliability
Cronbach's Coefficient Alpha (α)
Tau-equivalent Reliability
KR20

Reliability is how consistent test scores are. Think of your exam as a measurement instrument like a postal scale. If the scale displays a certain weight for a package on Monday, you would expect to have a similar weight on Tuesday. If your scale reading tells you that the package is 20% lighter the next day with no change to the package, then something is probably wrong with your scale. You need a consistent weight in order to pay the correct postage for the package. Likewise, if a measurement instrument of content mastery (your exam) is giving you one score on one day and a wildly different score for the same student on the next day (when the student's knowledge hasn't changed much), then something is wrong with the measurement instrument. It is not reliable. It is not providing any evidence of test-retest reliability.

Most instructors and students do not have the time to administer and take a test on multiple days just to compute reliability. What most people do is to estimate reliability from just one test administration. The mathematical techniques used to do this are basically tapping into how consistent questions are within the exam, which is a good proxy for test-retest reliability. In the testing industry, they call this internal consistency. Coefficient alpha (also known as α, Cronbach's coefficient alpha, and tau-equivalent reliability), and KR20 are two ways of estimating internal consistency reliability using only one exam administration. To learn why there are so many terms for alpha, why KR20 is called KR20, the difference between alpha and KR20, and when each is appropriate, see Chapter 4: Going Deeper (page 103). Rest assured that whatever the report is presenting is a sufficient estimate of reliability for your needs.

The values for reliability range from 0 to 1, with 0 meaning no reliability at all, and 1 indicating complete unity. Generally speaking, reliability on high-stakes tests tends to be very high, for example, in the .90s. Reliability in the .80s is respectable for many published tests, and .70 is considered adequate. Classroom exams tend to have lower reliability, sometimes in the .50s. Generally, you should try to take steps to improve reliability for values below .50 (Vegada, Karelia & Pillai, 2014).

Why is the reliability relevant?

Without evidence of reliability, a test is not able to give you consistent information about students' mastery of content. If one day, a test score tells you that a person is an A student but on the next day an equivalent test tells you that the student is failing (without any changes in the test or in the student's knowledge), then the test is giving you wildly different results with entirely too much measurement error. This could happen if you administered a test with merely one question on it. Form A would be one question, and Form B would be a different question. If the student happened to know the material covered in the question in Form A, they would be an A student. But if they didn't know the content associated with Form B, they would fail. With only one question, the scores could swing wildly. This is not desirable. You want your tests to be defensible and one requirement is that a test be acceptably consistent.

If the test has very low reliability, you might be able to increase the reliability by removing a poor-performing test question. You can determine which items are weak by looking at item discrimination (see page 31, Point-Biserial). The other approach is to increase the number of questions next time around. Generally, reliability can be improved by adding more high-quality questions to a test.

The other issue is this: you might *not* want your exam reliability to be super high. Here is why. The reliability estimate in your exam report will be based on one test administration. Remember that the techniques for estimating reliability using one test administration are really determining how consistent your test questions are to one another. This makes sense when creating exams that measure traits such as personality or intelligence, but for exams that measure subject content, you want test questions to be different from one another; the questions need to cover many topics. You can easily imagine cases where a student paid attention to the lecture on concept A but skipped the lab on concept B and never read the textbook section on concept C. For this student, test performance on test questions across the entire exam will not be consistent, and that's ok. There are general trends though. Good students tend to do well overall and poor students do not, especially on difficult material.

The goal then is to aim for a reliability that is high enough to be defensible (higher than .50) without sacrificing breadth of content or making the exam excessively long.

Standard Error of Measurement (SEM)

With any test, there is some degree of measurement error. Even when monitoring the speed of a car with a speedometer, there is measurement error. Government regulations ensure that car manufacturers keep this error within certain limits, for example, within 5% (meaning the actual speed must be within the range of 2.5% above or 2.5% below the reading on the speedometer).

Likewise, with tests, publishers give a range of where a true test score lies, which is a set number of points above or below the observed score. This reported number is the standard error of measurement or SEM.

The SEM is in reference to the scale of the test. For example, the SEM for a science test, which has a range of 0 to 100 possible points, might be 3. This means if Maria scored an 88, then the likelihood that her true score is 88 +/-3 (somewhere between 85 and 91 points) is .68. See Chapter 4: Going Deeper to understand the .68 part (page 108).

Why is the SEM relevant?

The SEM gives you another way to gauge a test's precision. A test with a small SEM is providing more scoring precision than a test with a large SEM. Drawing on the example above, if the SEM for the science test were much larger, such as 10, then Maria's true test score would be somewhere in the range of 78 to 98. If using a grading framework from the US where 70s are often Cs, 80s are Bs, and 90s are As, her true score could potentially be anywhere from a C to an A (a true score is what the student knows in truth. You can never know what a true score is, so you have to make do with an observed score). A true score somewhere in the range of a C to an A is not very precise. In contrast, a test with an unrealistic but phenomenal SEM of 1 would place Maria's true score somewhere between 87 and 89, a consistent B+.

Unfortunately, because different tests have a different number of possible points, there are no set thresholds for what your SEM should be. In general, if your SEM is more than 12% of the range of your scale (for example, if your SEM is more than 12 for a test with 0 to 100 possible points or more than 2 for a test with 0 to 20 possible points), then you might want to focus energy on reducing the SEM of future tests.

The goal then is to try to create tests with the smallest SEM possible given practical constraints. One way to do this is to increase the number of questions in the test (not just any questions, but high-quality questions). This approach is the same for increasing the test's reliability because there is a mathematical relation between a test's reliability and SEM. If you are mathematically minded and want to see the equation, go to Chapter 4: Going Deeper (page 111).

Percent Students Answered Correctly
p-value

For each test question, Item Analysis Reports usually present the percentage of students who selected each answer choice. The exam-analysis service takes the number of students who selected Choice A, for example, and divides by the total number of students who took the test. This will result in a proportion with values from 0.00 to 1.00. To make a percent, this number is then multiplied by 100 and a % sign is tacked on.

When this computation is done for the correct choice, and the proportion is reported, it is often referred to as a p-value, where p is the proportion of students who answered the question correctly.

The p-value is an indicator of how difficult a test question is. If the p-value is high (most students got it right), then the question is easy; if the p-value is low, then the question is hard. Most professionals target questions that are in the range of .30 to .90 (U Wisconsin, 2020). If your system flags problematic items, slightly different thresholds may be used, but the ideas are the same. An ideal p-value for a multiple-choice item with four choices is .74 (Lord, 1952).

Why is the p-value relevant?

A test that is designed to measure content mastery needs to cover a broad range of topics, and ideally it needs to present questions that range in difficulty. A student who has mastered content should not only be able to restate information but to apply it to real-life situations, synthesize concepts, and problem-solve.

Given these learning objectives, a test needs to offer students the opportunity to show higher-level thinking skills in a testing situation. When the level of thinking varies across questions, so does the question difficulty.

For tests of content mastery, it is okay to have an occasional easy question that all students answer correctly, especially if it is covering critical content. However, if most students can answer almost all questions right, then the test may not be probing deeper levels of comprehension.

Questions that 90% or more of your students answer correctly are most likely too easy. Questions that only 30% or fewer get right are most likely too hard. If presenting multiple-choice questions with four choices, then 25% answering correctly is guessing behavior. Test publishers aim for questions in the range of 30% to 90% because these questions provide you with the most information about student performance. However, in the classroom, a handful of easier items is expected. In general, I rarely recommend deleting a question from a test solely because of difficulty. There are always opportunities to improve the collection of items on the next exam.

Knowing the range of difficulty levels of test questions can help you understand whether or not the test as a whole was too easy, too difficult, or provided a nice variety of difficulty levels. This information can guide decisions about which style of items to bring forward into future exams.

Point-Biserial

r_{pb}

When analyzing exam questions, there are generally two metrics that tell you how well the question is functioning. The first is difficulty, which is quantified by the percent of students answering the question correctly (or p-value), as described in the previous two pages. The second is how well the question can discriminate students who know the material on a test from those students who do not.

There are different ways of quantifying a question's discrimination. One approach is to try to determine how well the question relates to overall content mastery. Generally, if a question relates strongly to mastery, then students who have mastered most of the content will tend to get the question right and students who are struggling will get it wrong. So how can you tell which student is which? A good proxy for content knowledge, if you are just looking at one test, is the overall test score. So, to quantify discrimination, many test publishers will correlate responses of the individual test question with overall test scores. Here is an example. Student 1 got the answer correct, so this response would be coded as 1. Student 2 got it right too, so the response would be 1 as well. Student 3 did not answer the question correctly, so this response is coded as 0. These coded responses are then correlated with overall test scores.

Table 1. Example Data for Point-Biserial

Students	Responses	Overall Test Score
Student 1	1	90
Student 2	1	95
Student 3	0	72
...		

Correlation = .41

Because one of the variables being correlated (the question response) is only 0s or 1s, the correlation is given a special name: point-biserial. Often researchers use r as the mathematical symbol for representing correlations, and so you will sometimes see a point-biserial referred to as r_{pb}, where r stands for the correlation and *pb* is an abbreviation for **point-biserial**.

With regard to interpretation, if the correlation is above .30, then the question is considered to have excellent discrimination. If the correlation is negative, then the discrimination is bad. In fact, high performing students are tending to get the question wrong, while students without mastery are getting it right. Somewhere in between 0 and .30 is a golden threshold that is appropriate for classroom tests, although the precise threshold is a matter of opinion.

Just as a side note, some systems correlate responses to a given item with total test scores as described above, while others will use total test scores minus the response to the item in question.

Why is the point-biserial relevant?

A point-biserial is an excellent way to quantify an item's ability to discriminate students based on their knowledge. Good discrimination tells you that the test question is functioning well and is able to distinguish between those students who know the content covered in the exam from those who do not.

Discrimination is so important that I recommend deleting a question from the test if its discrimination value is too low. If a question has a point-biserial that is negative, for example, then I would seriously consider computing scores without this question on the test. Of course, these issues need to be considered on a case-by-case basis. Often questions will have low point-biserials because they are too easy. When everyone is getting the question right, the point-biserial suffers. Sometimes negative point-biserials indicate that an item has been miskeyed and can be fixed easily by changing the answer key. Issues of practicality can also play a role if re-grading 400 exams is not feasible. However, some services will allow instructors to remove a question on a test and re-grade the exams with just a few clicks.

There are many reasons why a point-biserial might be low. Items that are too easy or miskeyed are just a few examples. Other reasons might be that a distractor is misleading, the question is biased against a particular subgroup, or the language in the question is ambiguous. Low point-biserials are a good opportunity to look closely at your questions and try to understand reasons for the response patterns (although honestly, sometimes it is difficult to figure out why a question is not functioning well).

The bottom line is that a point-biserial can tell you how well a test question is functioning and whether or not you should consider deleting it from your test, or at the least, revising it in future exams.

Reliability without an Item

Reliability without an item is a value reported by some systems, usually on the Item Analysis Report, that shows instructors what the reliability of the test would be if an item were removed.

Why is the reliability without an item relevant?
The quality of the items on an exam influences test reliability. So this value can help instructors identify poorly functioning items. In some cases, if an item is performing very poorly and the item is removed, the reliability can actually increase. This information can corroborate findings from other indicators of item quality including item discrimination.

Frequency of Each Choice
Low Performing Distractors

The frequency of each choice on a multiple-choice question is simply the number of students who selected each option (A, B, C, D or E). Sometimes this information is presented as percentages.

Why is the frequency of each choice relevant?

The frequency of each choice can provide you with two pieces of information. First, it can tell you about the difficulty of the question. If the frequency or percent associated with the correct answer is extremely high, then the question was easy. If it is low, the question was hard. This information is redundant with Percent Students Answered Correctly. Second, the frequency of each choice can give you information about which distractors students are choosing, which in turn tells you about the quality of the distractors.

For most questions, the selected choice with the highest number will be the correct answer, but not always. By itself, a low frequency or low percent for the correct answer does not dictate whether a question is good or bad. You might have a situation where the correct answer is selected by only 35% of the test takers. If these students are also the ones who did well on the test overall, then the question is actually functioning well; it is just a difficult question. The distractors are doing their job of luring lower-performing students into selecting these choices instead of the correct answer, which makes sense given that distractors are often inspired by student errors. The important thing to note about this situation is knowing *who* is getting the question right. This information is provided by discrimination values (for example, point-biserial as described above). If the discrimination for the question is good, then you know the expected people are the ones who are getting the answer correct, and the low frequency or percent of students selecting the correct answer is okay in this case.

When analyzing distractors, it is important to consider the number of students selecting a given distractor in concert with an item's discrimination. If distractor selection is high while the discrimination value for the item is low, then it could be the case that too many high-performing students are choosing this distractor. You can investigate further. Is the question miskeyed? Is there something about the distractor that is more appropriate as a choice than the correct answer? In contrast, if the number of students choosing the distractor is high and the discrimination value is also *high*, then the distractor is doing a good job of distracting the low-performing students – keep writing questions like this one.

Other information you can extract is whether or not students are enticed by the distractors. If the frequency of selecting a distractor is abysmally low, say less than 3% of the total responses, then the distractor is not doing its job of actually distracting from the correct answer. It is as if the distractor were not there. And in fact, it may not be worth your time writing third and fourth distractors if no students are selecting them. Once you identify neglected distractors, you can revise them for future exams or remove them. If too many questions show a pattern of one distractor with very low numbers and these distractors are the ones that took you a long time to write, you might use this information as evidence that you should move toward creating fewer distractors per question in general. Although the topic is debated in the field because of the trade-off with guessing probability (the fewer the choices, the higher the probably of a student being able to guess the correct answer), there are researchers who support fewer distractors, especially if one of them is not performing well (Lord, 1977; Rodriguez, 2005).

Group Percentages
Lowest 27% and Highest 27%

Group percentages show you how many students are getting a question correct. Different services will provide you with different groupings, but the main idea is to offer contrasting samples of students with regard to performance. In this way, you can see how the question is functioning for high-performers compared to low-performers.

A common way to create groups is to sort all students with regard to overall test performance and to select the top 27% and the bottom 27%. These groups are reflecting those students who showed mastery versus those who did not. Why 27%? Why not 25% or 30%? The reason is because a researcher recommended this amount for sensitivity and stability (Kelley, 1939). Keep in mind that almost all approaches for grouping students in this way will depend on how the entire class did in aggregate. In rare cases, all students in a class might have done well and the difference between the top 27% and bottom 27% is negligible, but generally speaking, with enough students, you will see a range of performances and will be able to use group percentages to glean important information at a glance.

Why are the group percentages relevant?

Group percentages provide you with a way of evaluating a question's discrimination. (Point-biserials are another way discussed above.) By looking at group percentages, you are able to determine whether or not a question can distinguish between those students who have mastered the test content from those who have not. The ideal pattern for a test question is having the percentage of students answering the question correctly be low for the bottom 27% and high for the top 27% as shown in Figure 4.

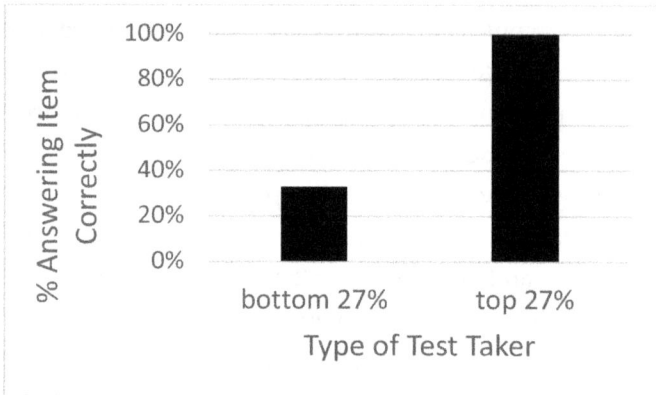

Figure 4. Ideal pattern for a test question when comparing performance of the bottom-performing 27% and top-performing 27%.

When a test question has around the same percentage for both groups, then the question is simply not providing you with much information regarding student performance. When the opposite pattern emerges (low for the mastery group and high for the non-mastery group), then a red flag should be raised. Something could be wrong with the question or the students' knowledge of the content covered in the question. In some cases, you might even consider removing the question from the test.

If your exam-analysis service is providing group percentages along with the question's point-biserial, you can cross reference the information. If the question looks good according to both metrics, then you can confidently conclude that it is performing well. If both are identifying a problem, you should address it. However, in some cases, a question could have a point-biserial below .30 but group percentages that seem reasonable. In other cases, the percentages might be a cause for concern but the point-biserial is above .30. Because group percentages and point-biserials are different metrics, they will not always send you the same messages about a question. Use your own judgment as to which questions might benefit from a review.

Discrimination Index (D)

Sometimes, item analysis reports will include something called the *discrimination index,* or D. This index quantifies the information from the top 27% and bottom 27% into a single number. (Again, the reason 27% is typically used is because of a paper written in 1939 by Kelley and is based on the D Index's sensitivity and stability.) The computation for the D Index involves subtracting the number of successes of the bottom-performing group from the number of successes of the top-performing group. The D Index ranges from -1 to +1 with values of .40 and above considered high discrimination and values below .20 as low (Ebel, 1965).

Why is the discrimination index relevant?

The discrimination index is yet another way to quantify an item's ability to discriminate students. This index was devised when instructors had to make discrimination computations by hand. Point-biserials were time-intensive without computing power, so the discrimination index was used more often. Now, with exam-analysis services that provide these numbers for you, point-biserials are more common.

Score Frequency

The score frequency is the number of occurrences of a given score on your test across the group of students who took the test. For example, if you had 100 students and 20 of them scored 50 points on your test, then the score frequency for 50 points would be 20.

Why is the score frequency relevant?

By itself, a single score frequency is not that interesting, but if you have score frequencies across all possible scores, then you can see the shape of the distribution. This is what a histogram is. A histogram shows you the distribution of scores graphically, which allows you to see where the center is, how wide the dispersion is, and whether or not there is a skew. See the next page for more on histograms.

Distribution / Histogram

In exam analysis, a distribution is a way to represent all the observed test scores from an exam. Often distributions are viewed as tables and graphs. A common way to graph a distribution is by using a histogram.

A histogram is a graph showing the frequency, which is simply the number of times that something occurred. For our purposes, the histogram is the frequency of test scores. Usually, histograms work best when scores are grouped together, so on the x-axis you will see that one bar represents the number of tests within a score range. On the y-axis is the frequency that a score within this range occurred. Figure 5 is an example of a histogram.

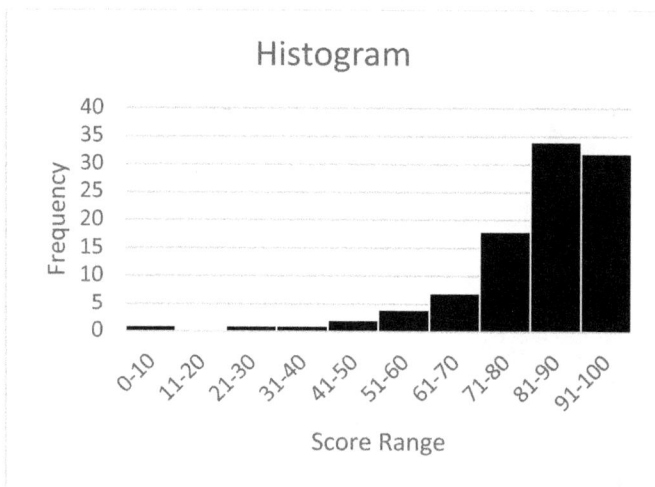

Figure 5. Example of a histogram.

The tallest bar in the histogram in Figure 5 tells us that there were 34 scores in the range of 81-90 on the test.

Why is the distribution/histogram relevant?

A distribution tells us where most students' scores appeared on the scale and how wide the span was. With histograms, we can understand a distribution at a glance and observe its shape. For example, a histogram shows us graphically if a distribution is symmetrical or skewed (spread out on one side more than the other).

For the histogram displayed in Figure 5, we see that most students had high scores. There was a negative skew, meaning that the distribution trailed off at the lower end of the scale where test scores were lower. From this graph, we know that although most students are grasping the material just fine, there are a handful of students with very low scores who need some extra support. When we understand the distribution, we can see how students performed as a group and can make decisions based on this information.

Cumulative Percent

Percent is the number of parts in every 100. We see percentages all of the time. If you have 10 students and 6 of them scored 100 on your test, then the percentage of students scoring 100 would be 60%.

6 students of interest / 10 students total = .60

.60 is a proportion. To make it a percent, multiply by 100 and tack on a percent sign:

.60 x 100 = 60%

Usually, you run into these terms in reports that are showing how students scored as a group. I'll assume that we are all familiar with percent, but what about cumulative percent?

Cumulative percent is the percent you have so far when summing them. Typically, counting starts with the lowest score. As an example, here is a table of scores including the frequency (tally), cumulative frequency, and cumulative percent:

Table 2. Frequency Table with Cumulative Percent

Score	Students	Frequency (f)	Cumulative f	Cumulative %
40	S1	1	1	10%
45	S2, S3	2	3	30%
50		0	3	30%
55	S4, S5	2	5	50%
60	S6-S10	5	10	100%

For the lowest score of 40, there was 1 student out of 10 with this score, or 10%.

Two students scored 45. Together, these two plus the one with a score of 40 give us a cumulative frequency of 3 and a cumulative percent of 30%.

For the score of 50, the frequency is 0. That's ok. The cumulative numbers are just themselves plus 0, so they don't change.

The scores continue this way until 100% is reached. Everything appears straightforward, but at this point, you may start protesting: "This is not what I'm seeing in my report." Indeed. In many reports, what is presented is the cumulative percent for occurrences below the current score. For example, they might say that the cumulative percent for a score of 55 is 30% (instead of 50%). If you are observing something like this and wondering why, see Chapter 4: Going Deeper (page 112).

Why is the cumulative percent relevant?

Cumulative percent values are sometimes used to graph distributions, but more often they appear in frequency tables in Score Distribution Reports. These tables include the frequency of test scores, and sometimes cumulative frequency and cumulative percent because this additional information can provide more context than just raw frequency numbers. For example, you can see generally where 50% lies and you can tell where large jumps in percentages occur. These patterns can tell you how students did as a group and whether or not performances were clustered together or were distributed across the scale.

Generally, in well-functioning tests, most students will score a bit above the middle score and will be spread across the distribution. Too many concentrated at the high end may indicate a test that is too easy. (Cumulative percentages will be low for most scores and then will jump abruptly for high scores.) Too many in the middle and at the low end may suggest that students were not prepared for the difficulty of the test. (In this pattern, percentages will increase fast and then will taper off slowly as scores increase.) Patterns of cumulative percent can guide creation of future tests, for example, by prompting you to write harder questions or by helping you customize instruction for students in your current class.

Percentiles and Percentile Ranks

Percentiles help with score interpretation, especially when you want to compare performance with a reference group. A percentile is a score at or below which a specified percentage of the scores fall. For example, if 50% of the test scores in your class have a score of 42 or below, then the 50th percentile is the score of 42. Some definitions say the percentile is the point *at or below* which a certain percentage of scores fall and other definitions say it is the value *below* which a percentage of scores fall. The difference has to do with the way people treat a score (as an integer or an interval range). For your purposes, just know that the percentile helps you understand where a score falls among a group.

A percentile is a point on the scale of your test. Most of the time, however, you are not looking for a score; you already have a list of scores. What you really want to know is: For each score, what is the percentage of scores at or below it. This is called the percentile rank. Often the terms *percentile* and *percentile rank* are used interchangeably. Really what you are looking at in these reports is a percentile rank.

Why are the percentile ranks relevant?

The main purpose of reporting a percentile rank is to help with score interpretation. The percentile rank provides information about where a score falls compared to scores from the rest of the group. If a student scores a 42 on a test and the percentile rank of this score is 50, then you know that the student's performance when compared with the rest of the group was average. Importantly, this information only tells you how the score compared to scores from the group; it does not tell you how much material the student understood since high scores or low scores could have a percentile rank of 50 depending on whether the students you are comparing to were skilled or not.

Percentile ranks can help guide your future test creation and instruction. Ideally, you want the majority of students to master most of the content on the exam, but you do not want all the scores to be at the ceiling of the scale. (In this case, percentile ranks will be low for most scores and then jump up at the high end of the scale.) Here, you might want to create more difficult test questions for future exams. Conversely, you do not want most of the students missing the majority of the content because this shows that the students are not prepared for the difficulty of the test. (Here you will see the progression of percentile ranks increase rapidly at the low scores on the scale and then more gradually at the high scores.) If you are seeing this pattern, then students might need a review of the content.

Z-Scores / Standard Scores

Z-scores are test scores that are standardized, meaning they are converted to a standard scale that tells you how far the score is from the group average (mean). For z-scores, the average is always set to 0. Scores below average are negative, and scores above average are positive. Scores are transposed to z-scores with reference to how many standard deviations the score is from the mean. Generally, z-scores range from -3 to 3. To get more information about how to interpret z-scores, see Chapter 4: Going Deeper (page 113).

Why are the z-scores relevant?

Z-scores can tell you which scores are far from average in either direction. From a grading perspective, they can be useful in helping instructors grade on a curve. To get more information on how to do this, see page 73 (Grading on a Bell Curve).

Bringing It All Together

At this point, you have been introduced to terms commonly appearing in exam analysis reports. Although it is important to understand each concept, it may feel as if there is so much information that it is hard to know where to begin applying any of it to your own exams. The goal of the next chapter is to bring all of these concepts together into the actual process of analyzing your exams using the UGIFT framework (Understanding, Grading, Instructing, Future Testing).

CHAPTER 3:

Implementing the UGIFT Approach

This chapter bridges the concepts presented in exam-analysis reports with action. To do this, we will rely on the UGIFT method presented in Chapter 1.

UGIFT
Understanding
Grading
Instructing
Future Testing

The UGIFT process will be described in detail using an example test and the information presented in three common reports: Summary Report, Item Analysis Report, and Score Distribution Report.

Before you begin, it might be a good idea to locate a copy of the exam for your reference and the test blueprint (if you created one). A blueprint is a document that specifies the construct to be tested (the ability you want to measure), the major content areas to be addressed by the test items, the number of items requiring different levels of difficulty or levels of thinking (cognitive level), and often the grading structure. Because examples help to make the explanations concrete, I created an example psychology exam. The blueprint for the exam is shown below.

Test Blueprint for Basic Psychology Exam

Intended Use of the Test: The purpose of the test is to determine to what degree test takers understand basic concepts in the field of psychology.

Examinees: [Usually this will be students in your class.] A total of 23 people with a range of educational backgrounds in psychology, from no background to PhDs in psychology.

Test Duration: [Usually this will be a class period.] Given that the administration is online, the test is designed to be timed so that answers cannot be researched. With 12 questions timed at 20-30 seconds, it is intended take about five minutes.

Scoring: There will be one point awarded per item. The test consists of 12 items, so the total number of possible points is 12. Skipped items are coded as incorrect.

High scores on the test are intended to be interpreted as an indicator of proficiency in basic psychology content, while low scores suggest little knowledge of the domain.

Topics	Percent of Test	Total # of Items	Cognitive Level		
			Low	Mid	High
Neuroanatomy	8-9%	1	1		
Learning	8-9%	1			1
Cognition	25%	3		1	2
Memory	8-9%	1		1	
Development	16-17%	2	1	1	
Personality	8-9%	1		1	
Social	16-17%	2		2	
Quantitative Methods	8-9%	1	1		
TOTAL	100%	12	3	6	3
1 point per question = 12 points					

The test questions and answer choices are displayed in Appendix A. I purposefully included a few items with structures and answer choices that are known to perform less effectively from a psychometrics perspective in order to demonstrate how problems can be detected in the item analysis process. These elements were an item with a choice of "none of the above," and a different item with a choice of "all of the above." Other problems were uncovered post hoc as a part of the item analysis process.

In the example, there were 12 total possible points. Presumably, your exam will be worth more. It is important to refresh your memory on the number of points possible because this defines the scale of your test. What do we mean when we talk about a scale? A scale is simply the ordered values used in your measurement. In academic environments, you are measuring some latent trait in your students' heads. Usually, this trait is mastery of content in a particular subject domain, such as psychology or chemistry. Your actual measurement is the number of points earned on a test. The scale of the test is the lowest possible score value (usually 0) to the highest possible score value (in our example, 12). In this case, the scale is 0 to 12 with each interval being one point. Even if not strictly true, the point values on tests are treated as if they are on an interval scale, where the interval between two points is equal no matter where you are on the scale. For example, the interval between 1 and 2 is the same as the interval between 11 and 12. This is not the case on all scales, but it is usually the assumption for classroom tests. The scale is important because statistics such as the average and standard error of measurement will be reported in reference to the test's scale.

Now that you have a copy of the test and the test blueprint, it is time to start looking at those reports.

UGIFT: Understanding the Overall Picture

The first component in the UGIFT approach is Understanding; namely, getting an overview of how your students did on the exam.

Step 1: Read the Summary Report
The goals of reading the Summary Report are twofold: (1) to understand the overall performance of students on the exam and (2) to evaluate the test's reliability (if reliability is reported).

Get an overview of student performance

Overall class performance is one of the first things you will want to review: Did everyone ace the test? Did everyone fail it? Was there a range?

First look at the class average (mean) and see where the value falls on the scale of your test. In our example, the average was 7.2 on a scale from 0 to 12. So, the average percent correct was 60%. This is a reasonable result given that people hadn't studied for the exam.

If the average is near the high score, then most students aced the test. In fact, the test might be too easy. If the mean is near the middle of the scale, then most students were awarded only half the possible points. This might indicate that the students did not learn the material, or at least they did not show their learning. Sometimes instructors consider curving grades when the average is extremely low. This depends on the department and instructor's grading philosophy. For multiple-choice tests with mostly four choices, an average somewhere between the high and middle score on the scale indicates that the students learned an adequate amount of the content and that the test was able to measure this learning. In our example, the average is a bit above the middle score of the scale, which is reasonable.

Now look at the median. Is it close to the mean? For the psychology test, the median was 8. If the median and mean are close, then the distribution might look something like a bell curve. If the mean and median are far apart on the scale, then the distribution of scores is most likely skewed in one direction or the other. This isn't bad; it just means that more people are clustered around a point on the scale that is not the middle. You can take a peek at the score histogram to see the distribution visually. Usually, the histogram appears on the Score Distribution Report. Figure 6 shows the histogram of scores for the psychology test.

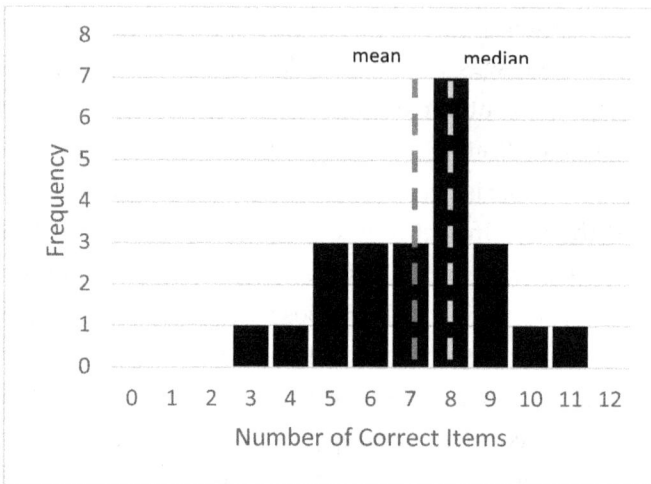

Figure 6. Histogram of scores on the psychology test. The mean is 7.2 and the median is 8.

As you can see from Figure 6, there are more people spread out across the lower point values. This means that the distribution is a bit negatively skewed. When this happens, the mean will be less than the median because the mean will get pulled down by the low scores.

There is no action at this point. Right now, you are simply getting a feel for the distribution of scores.

Look at the high score and the low score. Is there a big difference? For the psychology test, the high was 11 points and the low was 3, which is a big range. If the difference is large, then there is significant variability in student performance. If the high and low scores are close to one another, then students performed similarly. This information will become important in later steps when considering how to customize your instruction for this particular group of students.

Now compare this finding with the information from the standard deviation. Is the standard deviation more than 10% of the high score on the scale? In our example, the standard deviation was 1.90, about 16% of the scale (1.90 stdev / 12 total = 0.16, or 16%.) If the standard deviation is more than 10% of the scale, then there is a good amount of spread. This just means that students' scores tended to be distributed across the scale as opposed to clustered together. If the difference between the highest test score and lowest test score is large, then these two pieces of information (range and standard deviation) are giving you consistent information. If the range is large but the standard deviation is small, then it could be that an outlier or two are causing the range to be high. Again, there is no action. You are just understanding the distribution right now. File this information away – it will become useful in later steps when planning your future instructional objectives and upcoming exams.

Personally, I would not spend too much time analyzing variance. The standard deviation should give you everything you need at this point.

Now that you have a feel for the distribution of scores from the summary information, you can move on to reliability if these statistics are presented in the report.

Understand the test's reliability

Again, reliability is how consistent a test is. If the students were to be retested, would they get scores similar to the first test? With a reliable test, the answer would be yes. You want your tests to be defensible and one requirement is acceptable reliability.

Look at the reliability statistic provided. It could be called KR20 or Cronbach's coefficient alpha (or a subset of these words). The statistic should have a range from 0 to 1 and will usually be a decimal. For the example psychology test, the reliability is .40. As a rule of thumb, aim for a reliability of .50 or greater.

Often you will observe a low reliability if the scores on a test are all very high. A restricted range of scores can cause this to happen. The reason for the low reliability for the example psychology test could be the small number of items or it could be that a few of the items are of poor quality (or both).

When reviewing the reliability, simply get a feel for the information so that you can use it in a later step. The main point to remember is the answer to this simple question: Is reliability something that I will need to improve in a future test – yes or no? For our example test, the reliability is below .50, so the answer is yes.

Reliability information can be corroborated with the standard error of measurement (SEM), if provided. Again, SEM defines how much measurement error there is in a test. The smaller the SEM, the more precision. Usually, small SEMs will co-occur with high reliability values because they are mathematical related. In general, if your SEM is more than 12% of the range of your scale, then make a mental note that you should pay attention to this in a future step. For the psychology test, the SEM was 1.5, or about 13% of the scale. This means that there is a 68% chance that someone who scored an 8 has a true score between 6.5 and 9.5 (if a lot of people took the test). On such a short test, the SEM could be better.

With this, you have completed the first step of UGIFT. You now have a better understanding of the student score distribution and the general precision of the test. It is now time to move on to Grading.

UGIFT: Grading the Exams

The second component in the UGIFT approach is Grading the Exams. This involves Steps 2 and 3.

Step 2: Read the Item Analysis Report
An important step in grading is to ensure that all the items are functioning as intended. The answer key for each item should be available from the Item Analysis Report, so you can double check that all items were keyed correctly.

Along these lines, you can look at the percentage of students answering each question correctly. This percentage tells you how difficult the item is. When the percentage is high, the item is easy; when it is low, the item is very difficult. Just because the percentage is low does not automatically mean that there is a problem, but it is often an indicator that there is an error in the answer key. I have discovered many miskeyed items this way.

The items in the example psychology test had the following p-values (proportion of students answering the item correctly), which indicate how difficult the items were.

Table 3. Difficulty of Items in Example Psychology Test

Item #	p-value	Description
8	.87	easy
9	.87	easy
10	.83	easy
11	.74	ideal
12	.74	ideal
1	.65	somewhat difficult
7	.61	somewhat difficult
6	.57	somewhat difficult
2	.48	difficult
3	.39	difficult
5	.26	extremely difficult
4	.17	extremely difficult

The description ranges are as follows: 0% to 30% correct is considered extremely difficult because these numbers reflect guessing behavior or worse performance. 31% to 50% is difficult, 51% to 70% is somewhat difficult, 71% to 80% is an ideal range with Lord (1952) establishing that 74% is ideal for multiple choice items with four choices, 81% to 90% is easy, and 91% and above is extremely easy. Different types of items such as true/false or multiple-choice questions with a different number of choices will affect where you might place the boundaries of these ranges. Also, different grading services will use different thresholds. This example is just for illustration.

Because the p-values for Items 4 and 5 were so low I double-checked the answer key, but I did not detect any miskey problems. I deferred judgment on these items until reviewing item discrimination.

Determine if any items need to be eliminated from the exam

As a general rule of thumb, I do not recommend deleting questions from a classroom test just because they are extremely easy or difficult. When you do a more thorough analysis of the items with future tests in mind, you can come back to the percentage of students answering the item correctly and try to optimize these values in future tests.

Next, look at the numbers that tell you about item discrimination. One of the most common is the point-biserial (r_{pb}). If the point-biserial is negative, then this tells you that the students who are performing well on the test overall are getting this item wrong while the students who are not doing well are getting it right. First, check for any errors in the answer key. If there are no errors, consider if there are other potential correct answers. (Sometimes students might view a distractor in a certain way in which it could be interpreted as correct.) If you cannot make any adjustments to the answer key, then consider removing this item from your test. Nothing is an absolute, so decide if this action makes sense, but please do consider it. The statistics for this item indicate that the item is functioning poorly and test validity suffers when tests have poor items.

The items in the example psychology test had the following point-biserials, which indicate how well items can discriminate students according to their content knowledge.

Table 4. Discrimination of Items in Example Psychology Test

Item #	Point-Biserial	Description
12	.63	good
10	.53	good
9	.51	good
8	.51	good
6	.50	good
2	.46	good
1	.45	good
7	.45	good
5	.26	fair
3	.16	fair
4	.02	low
11	-.05	negative

There was one item on the test with a negative point-biserial. The difficulty for this item was .74, so difficulty was not the problem. Looking at the text, this item had a choice of "all of the above." Research has found that students can select "all of the above" without even reading the question and have a high chance of getting the answer correct (Mueller, 1975; Poundstone, 2014).

Sure enough, the answer for this item was "all of the above." This means that low-performing test takers who did not know the content could have easily guessed the answer.

Response patterns based on percentages from the top-performers and bottom-performers corroborated our observations from point-biserials. In Item 11, a large percentage of test takers in the high group chose "all of the above," but even more low-performers selected it. Clearly, the item did not do a good job of distinguishing these two groups. This item is a candidate for removal.

Item 4 did not have a negative discrimination, but the point-biserial was almost zero, which is not good. The difficulty of this item was extremely low at .17. Items with extreme difficulties in either direction can cause the discrimination to be low. Analysis of the content for this item revealed several problems. First, the item was worded in the negative, "Which is NOT ..." Negative wording adds unnecessary complexity and cognitive load and has been shown by researchers to be more difficult than items with positive wording (Cassels & Johnstone, 1984; Dudycha & Carpenter, 1973). In addition, the last choice for this item was "none of the above," which has been associated with higher difficulty and lower discrimination (Forsyth & Spratt, 1980; Mueller, 1975; Wesman & Bennett, 1946). Combined, these two elements created a double negative, which is such poor form that it is not even addressed in the literature. It is no surprise that this nightmare of an item had an extreme difficulty of .17 and an abysmal discrimination of .02.

Again, group percentages corroborated point-biserial results. For Item 4, 17% of high-performers selected the correct answer, while the majority chose "none of the above." For the low-performers, about an equal number selected each choice, indicating guessing behavior. Often with "none of the above" items, experts will reject the correct answer because of technical details and resort to the "none of the above" choice. This phenomenon might be causing the response pattern here, with most high-performers resorting to "none of the above." This item is another candidate for removal from the test.

Item 3 had a fair discrimination value of .16. This discrimination does not warrant removal but should be investigated.

The following is the text of the item:

Which is an example of a top-down process?

A. seeing basic features of a letter such as a horizontal line

B. expecting what the last word in a sentence will be

C. separating sounds into individual words

D. detecting a grammatical error in written text

The text for this item did not have known problems such as negative wording, "all of the above," or "none of the above." Because the problem was not obvious, the text of the item was analyzed in more detail. A top-down process is one in which higher-level knowledge and expectations guide processing of information. In contrast, bottom-up processes are those in which basic units are processed first without involvement from background knowledge or context. Given this, we can review the choices. A is an incorrect response because the act of processing features of a letter is a canonical example of a bottom-up process. B is the correct answer. (A top-down process would allow someone to anticipate a word). C describes a bottom-up process where sounds are built up into words. D is actually ambiguous. Grammar is in between printed letters and meaning, so its position in the bottom-up and top-down hierarchy is equivocal. Experts taking the psychology test seemed to agree. Responses from the top 27% of the test takers were analyzed. Of these, 50% chose the correct answer and 33% selected the ambiguous D. These two answers accounted for 83% of the group. Contrast these responses with the bottom 27%. For these low-performing test takers, 33% selected (guessed?) the correct answer and none chose D. If we consider that maybe D could be a correct choice as well, how do the statistics change? With two correct choices, the difficulty moves from .39 to .61 (toward the direction of ideal difficulty) and the discrimination increases from .16 to .31 (from fair to good). So, a deeper analysis of this item revealed a potential improvement with an adjustment to the answer key. This adjustment was only possible because one of the choices was ambiguous. If all of the distractors were clearly wrong, then an adjustment to the answer key would not have been justified.

To summarize our findings, we identified two items with problematic discrimination. We investigated further and found that for one item, too many low-performers chose the correct answer of "all of the above," and for the other, too many high-performers chose the distractor "none of the above." Both items were placed on a list for potential removal. We also found one item with fair discrimination that could be improved with an answer key adjustment. In all three examples, looking at group performance corroborated findings from point-biserials and allowed us to understand what was happening in more detail.

The steps are the same for any analysis when considering discrimination:

- Identify items with low discrimination (less than .15 is a reasonable threshold but your service may use a different one).
- Look at the response patterns of high-performers compared to low-performers.
- Review the content of the item.
- Try to understand why discrimination was poor.
- Take steps to adjust the answer key if sensible. If necessary, remove the item.

Because group percentages and point-biserials are different metrics, they will not always yield consistent results. With this ambiguity, you will have to rely on personal judgment. You might consider writing down your reasoning for the decisions you make regarding keeping or discarding items in case of challenges or the need to trace your own logic at a later date.

Some exam-analysis services will provide information about how removing an item will affect the overall reliability of the exam. You can use this information along with the other discrimination values to reinforce any decisions about keeping or removing items.

Re-grade if needed

If the answer key needs to be adjusted or any items removed because of poor performance, re-grade all student tests. For fairness, scoring should be standardized, which means that any decisions made for one exam should apply to all. Afterward, scores will be different, so restart the UGIFT process from Step 1. Usually, eliminating one item does not affect scores wildly so the review of the Summary Report should go much quicker the second time around.

Sometimes you will find that removing one or more items then bumps other items beyond the thresholds. Use personal judgment here. It is reasonable to stop a cascading effect if too many items continue to be removed from the exam. Usually, you will start to see decreases in exam reliability if too many items are removed. This is an indicator to stop the process and retain the remaining items.

For our example test, we eliminated two items and rekeyed one. This changed the mean to 6.5 out of 10, and the median shifted to 7. Importantly, reliability improved from .40 to .61. The SEM decreased from 1.5 to 1.3, but this could still be improved in a later test by adding more items. Item difficulties ranged from .26 to

.87, and discrimination values were all .20 or above (which is great). Overall, tightening up the test by removing and fixing poor-functioning items improved the statistics of the test.

Step 3: Read the Score Distribution Report

At this point in the process, you are still focused on grading exams and getting scores back to your students. The Score Distribution Report is packed with information, but for now, we will focus only on your grading efforts. Given this, the extent that you use the Score Distribution Report will depend heavily on your grading philosophy.

With regard to grading, there are several different approaches you can take, and your choice will depend on your personal grading viewpoint as well as mandates and suggestions from your institution's department. A common approach is to grade on a criterion, that is, some agreed-upon standard. For example, in many schools in the US, getting 90% correct out of the total possible points implies that a student has mastered almost all of the content on the exam and canonically is given the grade of A. When grading on a criterion, if all students scored 90%, they would all receive As (or whatever the appropriate mapping is).

When criterion-style grading is used, the instructor may add group information such as percentile rank to facilitate score interpretation. The Score Distribution Report usually provides this information.

Reporting Percentile Rank

Reporting percentile rank is straightforward because most exam analysis services provide it without any need for computation. Keep in mind that the service might use the label percentile. All you have to do then is to report this number along with the student's grade. Be prepared to explain to students what the percentile rank means. Again, it is the percentage of scores that are the same as the student's score or lower. Traditionally, percentile ranks range from 1 to 99. An example frequency table that might appear on a Score Distribution report with percentile ranks is provided in Table 5.

Table 5. Frequency Table from Example Test

Points	Percent Correct	Frequency	Percent of Group	Percentile Rank
0	0%	0	0%	1
1	10%	0	0%	1
2	20%	0	0%	1
3	30%	2	9%	4
4	40%	4	17%	17
5	50%	2	9%	30
6	60%	1	4%	39
7	70%	7	30%	57
8	80%	3	13%	78
9	90%	2	9%	87
10	100%	2	9%	99

For a student scoring 8 points, you could report the raw score (8 points), the percent correct (80%), the corresponding letter grade (B, if using criterion-referenced scoring), and the percentile rank (78). By adding a percentile rank of 78 to the score information, you share with the student the fact that 78% of the people in the group had a score of 8 or less. If scores are generally low, reporting percentile ranks can give students a different perspective regarding their grade.

In contrast to a criterion-referenced approach, group-referenced grading or quotas take into account the scores of other students in the class. The group might also include students from several classes or within an entire department. Sometimes, even historical data are considered. Using group performance for grading can often be a source of student complaints, but the reason for it is to control for grade inflation, especially when different instructors are teaching the same course and are grading with different levels of leniency. This approach is often implemented in competitive medical, law, and business schools. Understanding the score distribution is vital for this style of grading and the Score Distribution Report can aid in the process of grade assignment.

Sometimes an instructor will start with criterion-style grading but then will discover from exam analysis that scores are collectively low and will choose to boost grades (aka curve grades). There are many ways to do this and the Score Distribution Report can help with these efforts as well.

If your grading scheme does not involve comparing to a group or curving grades, then feel free to skip to the next step in the UGIFT process.

Use information to assign grades

This section describes techniques for using information in the Score Distribution Reports for assigning grades.

Grading on a Bell Curve or Using Quotas

When grading on a bell curve or using quotas, you are basically ranking students by their performance on the test, and then assigning grades based on percentages inspired by the bell curve or established quotas. All you need for this exercise is a list of scores ranked, and the frequency or percent of students associated with each score, which many Score Distribution Reports provide.

When using this approach, it is a good idea to establish at the beginning of the course what percentage of each grade will be assigned so that expectations have been set. For example, a rather strict but symmetrical grade distribution might be the following:

Option 1

A	7%
B	24%
C	38%
D	24%
F	7%

This is based on the normal distribution and the percentage of students within each section shown in Figure 7.

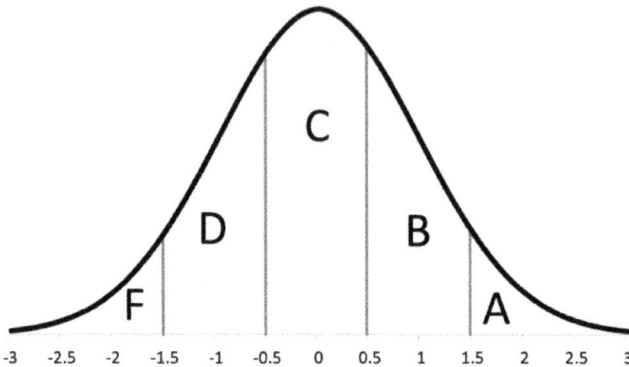

Figure 7. Using the normal distribution to determine grade assignment (Option 1 of many).

The numbers on the x-axis are the number of standard deviations above and below the mean of 0. If there were 100 students represented in this distribution, then given what we know about the normal distribution, 38% would be in section C, which is between one half of a standard deviation below the mean and one half above it.

This is not the only way to divide up the normal distribution. You could choose to set the middle between the C and B boundary as in Figure 8.

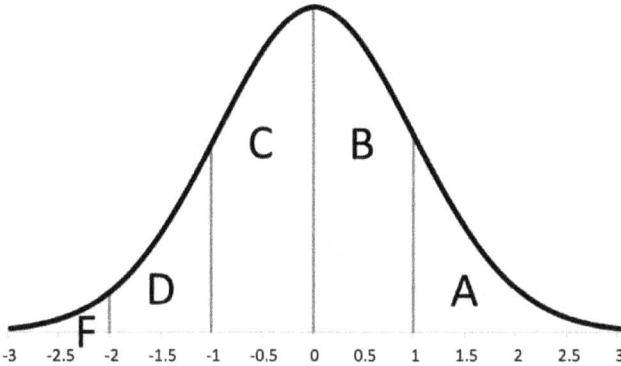

Figure 8. Using the normal distribution to determine grade assignment (Option 2 of many).

The sections from Figure 8 would result in the following percentages for each grade assignment:

Option 2
A   16%
B   34%
C   34%
D   13%
F   3%*

* The percent for F is actually 2, but because of rounding the total would not add up to 100%.

Some educational departments might not follow the bell curve strictly but rather introduce quotas reflecting historical data. For example, a department might mandate that no more than 35% of a class be assigned a grade of A, and these quotas might trickle down into grade assignments for a classroom test.

Regardless of the exact percentages chosen, the technique of using percentages for assigning grades is the same. For our example, we will use Option 1: A= 7%, B = 24%, C = 38%, D = 24%, and F = 7%.

The technique involves looking at a frequency table and lining up the percentages as closely as possible to the ideal percentages. The frequency table for our example test is repeated below for convenience. For simplicity, this version of the table does not include raw scores with a frequency of 0.

Table 6. Frequency Table from Example Test

Points	Percent Correct	Frequency	Percent of Group	Percentile Rank
3	30%	2	9%	4
4	40%	4	17%	17
5	50%	2	9%	30
6	60%	1	4%	39
7	70%	7	30%	57
8	80%	3	13%	78
9	90%	2	9%	87
10	100%	2	9%	99

From Table 6, we see that the lowest earned score was 3 points, constituting 9% of the group. This is the lowest possible percent (aside from 0%), so we assign Fs to those tests with 3 points. Next, we assign tests with 4 points and 5 points a D. This comprises 26% of the group, which is close to our target of 24%. Then we assign Cs to tests with 6 or 7 points, which is 34%

compared to our target of 38%. Tests with 8 or 9 points together make up 22%, which is close to the 24% needed for Bs. Finally, those with a score of 10 are assigned As. Table 7 presents the final grade assignments.

Table 7. Final Grade Assignments for Option 1

Grade	Points	Frequency	Actual Percent	Target
A	10	2	9%	7%
B	8, 9	5	22%	24%
C	6, 7	8	34%	38%
D	4, 5	6	26%	24%
F	3	2	9%	7%

Our actual percentages lined up nicely with our targets. If we had chosen Option 2, the exercise would have been a bit more challenging. In that case, we would have tried different groupings as shown in Table 8.

Table 8. Grade Assignments for Option 2

Grade	Version A Points	Version A Actual %	Version B Points	Version B Actual %	Target
A	9, 10	18%	10	9%	16%
B	7, 8	43%	8, 9	22%	34%
C	4, 5, 6	30%	5, 6, 7	43%	34%
D	3	9%	4	17%	13%
F		0%	3	9%	3%
Total Absolute Difference from Target		22%		38%	

Here we came up with two grade assignment versions. The versions were then compared by computing the absolute difference between the actual and target percentages. Presumably in your test, student scores will be spread across more points allowing you to select percentages that are close to your targets.

If the Score Distribution Report includes z-scores, then you can make use of them for this exercise. A z-score (also called a standard score) is a transformed test score. A regular test score is on a scale based on the number of total points possible. When a test score is transformed to a z-score, it changes to the scale used for the normal distribution, with a mean of 0.

If your scores are normally distributed (meaning the score distribution is symmetrical and looks like a bell curve), then you can refer to the normal distribution to find the z-scores where you placed grade boundaries.

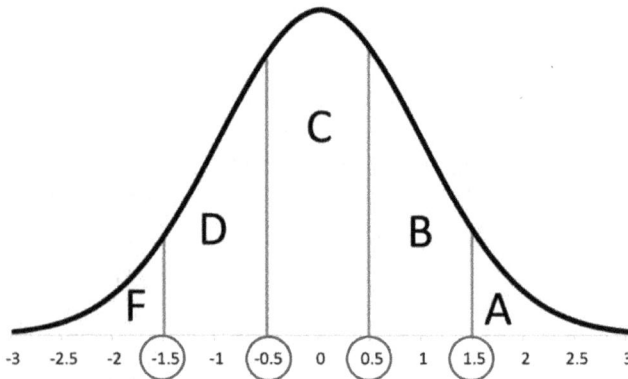

Figure 9. Z-scores associated with grade boundaries (Option 1 of many).

For example, in Figure 9, the boundary between grades A and B is a z-score of 1.5. For Option 1, z-score ranges associated with each grade are listed in Table 9.

Table 9. Grades Associated with Z-Score Ranges for Option 1

Grade	Percent	Z-Score
A	7%	Higher than 1.50
B	24%	0.51 to 1.50
C	38%	-0.50 to 0.50
D	24%	-1.50 to -0.51
F	7%	Lower than -1.50

Look up the z-score for each student and then find the appropriate range. For our example, the final grade assignments are listed in Table 10.

Table 10. Z-Scores and Grades for Example Test

Points	Z-Score	Grade
10	1.69	A
9	1.21	B
8	0.73	B
7	0.25	C
6	-0.23	C
5	-0.71	D
4	-1.19	D
3	-1.67	F

Results using the z-score method are identical to those derived from percentages. However, with Option 2, the assignments would be slightly different between the two methods. The reason for the difference is that the distribution is negatively skewed so when using z-scores, more tests are beyond one standard deviation below the mean.

When deciding which method to use for group-referenced grading (percentages versus z-scores), consider if you care more about preserving a certain percentage of As, Bs, Cs, Ds, and Fs (percentages method), or if you would rather emphasize how far a student is from the average score (z-score method).

If you prefer the z-score method, but z-scores are not provided, you can use a calculator or spreadsheet software to compute z-scores by hand. For details, please see Chapter 4: Going Deeper (page 113).

Curving Grades

So far, we have seen how percentile ranks can help with score interpretation and how frequencies and percentages can help with group-referenced grade assignment. Another place where the Score Distribution Report can be applied is when curving grades.

One technique is to look for gaps in the score distribution. For this approach, it is useful to reference a histogram. Our example psychology test does not give us a clear demonstration of gaps, so a different example histogram is presented. This one is from a test of English grammar with non-native speakers as test takers.

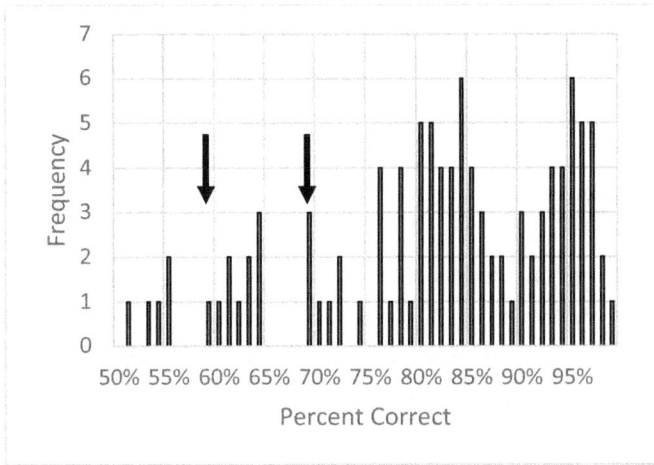

Figure 10. Histogram of percent correct on an English grammar test.

In Figure 10, there are two arrows. One appears at 59% correct and another at 69%. If using the canonical criterion-referenced grading scheme in the US (A: 90-100%, B: 80-89%, C: 70-79%, D: 60-69%, and F: 0-59%), the person who scored 59% correct would be assigned an F, even though there is a clear gap between this person's score and the cluster of other students with F grades. If adjusting grades by looking at gaps, then the person with 59% would be grouped with students who scored in the 60s and would be assigned a D. Likewise, the three students with 69% correct would be grouped with students who scored in the 70s because there is a clear gap between the performance of these students and those who scored soundly in the D range. The reasoning here is that the boundaries for each grade are based on tradition as opposed to more rigorous methods that look at the content of the test itself to determine more exact endpoints. Here the boundaries of the ranges are adjusted slightly given patterns in the distribution. Explicit gaps do not appear at boundaries for higher grades (C/B, and B/A), and therefore adjustments are not justified for those cut points.

Other curving techniques do not require much information from the Score Distribution Report. Two simple methods involve adding a set number of points to everyone's score. For these, you just need summary information, such as the mean, median or high score. For example, some instructors take the mean of the class and then shift it to where the instructor thinks the mean should be. Then everyone's test score is adjusted by that number of points. This shifting can be done with percent correct as well. In our example psychology test, the mean percent correct was 65%. If I wanted to curve grades, I might add 10 percentage points across the board. This would bring the average to 75%. One drawback of this is that the people with high scores would then have 110% correct. (Although they probably wouldn't complain.)

You could choose to use the median percent correct to do the same thing. The median is 70%. You could shift all scores up by 5 percentage points if you wanted the median to be 75% correct.

In a similar vein, some instructors take the high score and then add points to make it equal to the total number of points possible, and then the instructor adds this amount to all test scores. I recommend working with a mean or median instead because the highest score can sometimes be an outlier. When you are working with means and medians, you are dealing with the center of the distribution, which is a better representation of the performance of all students.

Other curving techniques involve ways of shifting such that the poor performers get a bigger boost than the high performers. These approaches do not rely on information from exam analysis; rather a formula is applied to each score. For example, some instructors take the square root of the percent correct to come up with an adjusted percent correct. For example, 80% would become

$$\sqrt{.80} = .89 = 89\%.$$

As described above, there are many ways to assign grades each with their pros and cons. Some make use of the Score Distribution Report and some do not. Whichever approach you choose, clearly document it and set student expectations early.

Now that you have the tools to assign grades, you are ready to move on to other steps in the exam analysis process that look toward the future.

UGIFT: Instructing Based on Performance

The third component in the UGIFT approach is Instructing Based on Performance. After the rush of returning grades has subsided, the work of understanding student performance and using it to guide instruction can begin. Even though the act of assigning grades is essential to your role as instructor and may be associated with high expectations and deadlines not felt with other steps in the process, these other steps can greatly enhance your effectiveness as a teacher. Probably the most important step is using the information from the exam reports to understand where your students are in their learning and customize instruction based on their performance.

Step 4: Reread the Score Distribution Report and Item Analysis Report

Information from both the Score Distribution Report and Item Analysis Report will be important for reflecting on student performance and areas where students did not master content. This information will be viewed from two different perspectives: for the group and for the content.

First, look at the Score Distribution Report and get a feel for the shape of the distribution. Visually, determine where the mode is (the mode is the highest point on the histogram or the point with the highest frequency). Using this visual cue along with the mean and median values, try to identify the score or range of scores the distribution centers around. If the center is sufficiently low, you might consider revisiting the most important material covered on the exam.

It is difficult to establish the exact threshold for deciding when to revisit content. Different tests have different scales, and student scores will be distributed in different ways, but generally, you want students as a group to master at least 70% of the content. This, of course, is an arbitrary percentage and a more thorough method can be used to identify a precise percentage for the exam in question. The method involves first imagining student performance that would be minimally acceptable for mastering the content on the exam, and then going through the exam item by item and determining the probability that the student would get each item correct. Then for each item, multiply the probability by the number of points possible for the item. For example, if you think the student would have a 60% chance of answering an item correct, and if the item is worth one point, then the expected number of points earned would be .6 of a point. (It is okay if it is not a whole number.) If the next item is worth 5 points and you think the minimally acceptable student would have a 40% chance of getting it right, the expected points for this item would be 2 (.40 x 5 points = 2 points). Summing these expected points across the entire test will give you a lower bound of what the raw score on the test should be. If the center of your distribution is below this score, then you know that your group of students is not mastering the material.

Next, evaluate the distribution to see if most students are clustered together. If so, then you can target your teaching for the average student in the class and you will reach most of them. If a few struggling students or a subgroup are performing lower than average, then you know that you have to make accommodations for a range of student abilities. In a histogram, struggling students will appear as a tail at the lower scores with the peak of the curve being at much higher scores (indicating that most students did just fine).

The non-native students taking an English grammar test provide an example of most students doing fine with a handful of struggling subgroups needing support. The histogram is repeated here.

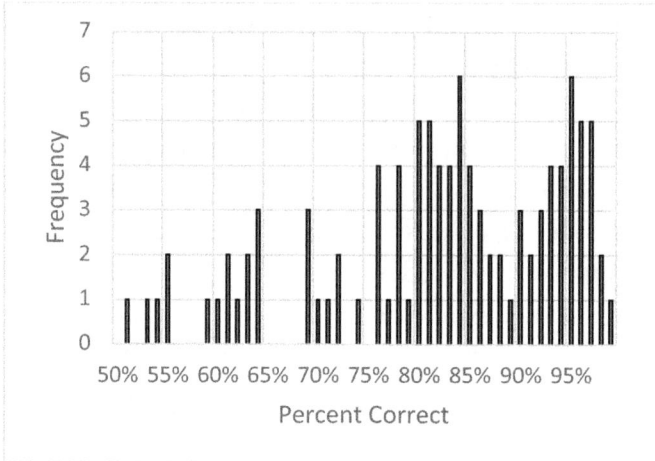

Figure 11. Histogram for an English grammar test.

This distribution is interesting because it has two modes. It appears that one group of students has very good mastery (84% correct) and another has outstanding mastery (95%). Meanwhile, there is a subgroup in the tail below the threshold of 70% correct needing support.

Of course, score distributions can take different shapes. If the distribution is lean and tall but the center is low, then all students might benefit from a review during class. If the tail is on the high end, but the center is low, then there are a few students mastering the content, but again most students might need further instruction. The standard deviation can corroborate these conclusions, but generally, the histogram will tell you the story of student performance.

Once you have determined the audience needing support (a few struggling students, a subgroup, or possibly the entire class), then you can switch over to the Item Analysis Report to understand the specific content areas that might need to be covered again. The quickest way to extract this information is by skimming the percent of students answering questions correctly and identifying those with low percentages.

Some services will place items in a grid depending on difficulty and discrimination.

Table 11. Item Analysis Grid

		Difficulty		
		Hard < .50	Medium .50 – .84	Easy > .84
Discrimination	Poor < .15	4	11	
	Fair .15 – .29	5		
	Good > .29	2	1, 3, 6, 7, 10, 12	8, 9

By focusing on items that functioned satisfactorily (fair or good discrimination) but that were hard, you can concentrate on the content areas that were most challenging. (You do not want to place too much emphasis on items that functioned poorly because they are giving you muddled information.) For our example psychology test, we see that test takers found Items 2 and 5 difficult, which corresponded to content on learning, cognition, and decision making. The appropriate audience might find a review of these topics beneficial.

Comparing against the blueprint, you can see if the difficult items were an artifact of cognitive level. Were students missing items because they were designed to be hard and involved higher-order reasoning, or were the difficult items associated with specific subtopics? Maybe there was an interaction between these things and students missed the items of a specific cognitive level on a specific subtopic. This kind of analysis can help you understand if you need to review material, formulate additional activities that exercise a certain way of thinking, or both. From our blueprint, we see that there were two content areas where we targeted higher-level thinking and those areas were learning and cognition. This tells us that not only is the content relevant, but that higher-level thinking skills might be an important area of focus as well.

Devise a plan for customizing instruction

After understanding which students need extra help and which content areas or thinking levels require extra attention, you can now pull everything together and envision how to customize your instruction.

Books and articles specializing in teaching offer many suggestions including the following:

- Identify different or supplementary resource material such as textbooks, articles, videos, and websites

- Introduce concepts using multiple modalities including audio and visual

- When presenting new concepts, take time to review and reinforce old concepts

- Try new methods of instruction such as learning by doing, team-based instruction, and projects

- Offer review sessions
- Provide more practice with higher-level thinking activities

- Build in more performance tracking between tests

- Give out practice questions

- Consider a revise-and-resubmit opportunity for additional points to emphasize learning

- Facilitate opportunities for self-assessment

- Suggest on-campus tutoring resources

(CTL, 2021; Mertler, 2003; Sindelar, 2003;)

Your planning involves not only how to address the learning of your current group of students, but how to adjust your approach the next time around, for example, devoting more time to specific topics.

Review individual performance

Meeting with struggling students individually can have a positive impact on future performance. By reviewing missed items, you can highlight content areas where development is needed and suggest individualized remediation.

To summarize the Instructing component of UGIFT, visually inspect the score histogram in the Score Distribution Report for information about how many students need support, and then use the Item Analysis Report along with the test blueprint to help you precisely locate areas in the curriculum that students need reinforced. Then devise a plan for customizing instruction. If meeting with individual students, review their missed items to understand general areas of development.

After you have a plan for how to refine your approach to instruction, you can now move forward to the last step in the UGIFT process that involves improving future tests.

UGI**FT**: Future Testing Improvements

The final component in the UGIFT approach is Future Testing Improvements. This component involves revisiting reports and attending to details regarding test performance.

Step 5: Reread the Summary Report

There are two purposes for reviewing the Summary Report. One is to remind yourself of the test reliability and the other is to think about test difficulty.

Make decisions regarding reliability

As mentioned previously, if the reliability of the test is low (and likewise, the standard error of measurement is high), then it may be worth trying to improve the precision of the test. One straightforward way of doing this is to increase the number of questions on the next test. This approach is not failproof since adding low-quality items will often not help. However, increasing the number of items is a good rule of thumb for improving reliability, and it is an easily actionable item.

If adding to the test length is not an option because of time constraints, then often replacing poor-performing items can help. Poor-performing items are usually those with low discrimination values. If high-mastery students are getting the item wrong, then the item may be performing poorly. Also, if everyone is getting the item right, metrics for item quality such as discrimination can suffer. Flagging these items now can help you avoid choosing similar items in future exams.

In our psychology test, for example, we could definitely add more items to improve reliability. The question often arises as to how many items are needed to increase the reliability to a desired level. There is an equation that can estimate the number you need. For more detail, see Chapter 4: Going Deeper (page 107). Or, you can use our online calculator:

www.intelliphonics.com → Resources → Number of Items

Make decisions about future test difficulty

In the Summary Report, revisit information about the general performance of the class. For this exercise, you might also refer to the score histogram most likely in the Score Distribution Report.

If the center score of the test (mean or median) was too high, then it could be that you have an extremely advanced group of students, the test was too easy, or a combination of these. You know your students best and can most likely ascertain which of these is true. You could be satisfied with the amount of content the students have learned and plan to write harder test questions that extend into high-order thinking the next time around.

If the center of the test was low, then the opposite potential reasons apply: the students need support, the test was too hard, or a combination of these. Ask yourself whether or not the questions were of the desired level. If yes, then the focus should be on how to bring the next group of students up to the challenge. If no, then it is possible that the test questions might need to be refined.

Knowing where students stand as a group can help you know whether or not you should adjust the difficulty of future exam questions. Once you have an idea of the desired direction of the exam difficulty, then you can analyze individual items to understand which question types to include or remove in future tests.

Step 6: Reread the Item Analysis Report

There are two goals for Step 6: (1) to compare performance with your test blueprint and (2) to make notes of item adjustments needed for future exams.

Compare item performance with the test blueprint

Presumably your test blueprint specifies how many items to write at different levels of difficulty/thinking for each subtopic. Now that you have exam data, you can compare your plan with the actual difficulty levels. Using the difficulties in the Item Analysis Report, you can categorize items into three bins: difficult (0% correct to 50%), medium (51% to 80%) and easy (81% to 100%). These category boundaries are just suggestions, so you can feel free to adjust them to your needs.

The example test blueprint on pages 54-55 specified three levels of question difficulty or cognitive level: low, mid, and high. Now, you can compare planned cognitive level with actual difficulty and see how many questions aligned with your plan. Table 12 shows a comparison for items in the example psychology test using all 12 items.

Table 12. Planned Cognitive Level Compared to Actual Difficulty in Example Exam

		Actual Difficulty			
		Easy	Medium	High	**TOTAL**
Cognitive Level	Low	1	2		**3**
	Mid	2	3	1	**6**
	High		1	2	**3**
	TOTAL	**3**	**6**	**3**	

The results are excellent. (I wasn't expecting them to look so nice actually). Even though there were some questions targeted for a certain cognitive level that resulted in a different difficulty level (for example, they were more difficult), there were an equal number that moved in the opposite direction (they were less difficult). So the effects washed out.

Consider making notes regarding which questions matched or did not match your expectations so that you can plan for next time. Were the easy items the ones that you intended to be easy because of content coverage, or were they unintentionally easy because of cues exploited by test-savvy students? Were the difficult items ones that you intended to be difficult or did these items have unforeseen problems such as unclear language or negative wording?

When thinking about techniques for how to make items easier or harder, focus on content. Resist the temptation to use mechanics that are known to degrade discrimination. For example, if you need more difficult items, you might be tempted to add some with "none of the above" because this choice makes an item more difficult, but resist. The discrimination will most likely suffer. Instead try techniques such as introducing higher-level thinking, making inferences, or synthesizing concepts.

Identify items or item types that need future revision

After you have analyzed difficulty level, you can focus on other features that suggest future item revisions. Two elements to consider are discrimination and distractors.

Review the discrimination values again. You did a first pass when determining if any items with low discrimination needed answer key adjustments or if any should have been removed from the test. In this pass, you can analyze those with fair discrimination (anything below .30) and see how to improve these items. Is the discrimination suffering because the item is too easy or too difficult? Is there another reason? What might make the discrimination better?

Sometimes, the reason is because the item is tapping into something else that has nothing to do with the content you are trying to teach. For example, if you inadvertently included a choice that a subgroup considered biased or taboo and students from this subgroup focused on this aspect of the item instead of the content, then the discrimination can suffer because you are distracting these students in unintended ways. (As a test taker, I have come across some surprising content in items that definitely should have been screened out.) In other cases, low discrimination is due to the fact that too many high-performers chose the wrong answer.

In our psychology exam, for example, Item 5 had a discrimination value of .26. This is not too bad, but it could be better. It turns out that this item was quite difficult and reflected guessing behavior (with a p-value of .26, which is basically chance performance). The following is the item text:

> Why are human estimates of likelihood often incorrect?
> A.   People misinterpret expected values.
> B.   People resist stereotypes.
> C.   People create faulty frequency distributions.
> **D.   People ignore the base rate.**

This question was drawn from research by Kahneman and Tversky (1973) with a correct answer of D. Other words related to math were used as foils in Choices A and C (expected value and frequency distribution) and another concept related to bias was incorporated in the Distractor B. Although these concepts are indeed taught in psychology, it might have been quite some time since hearing these terms for many. An analysis of the bottom-performers indeed showed that all options were selected (A 33%, B 17%, C 17%, D 33%) Basically, these test takers were guessing. For the top-performers, the selections were split 50/50. Half chose the correct answer D (base rate) and half chose C (frequency distribution). Because so many top-performers selected this choice, it was probably too tempting. A different distractor, possibly with less statistical jargon, might improve the discrimination.

Discrimination values for all other items were good.

Now you can shift gears and instead of finding poorly-functioning items, you can look at all items and focus on distractors. Some distractors may not be getting enough traction, even if the item is performing well according to item discrimination statistics. Information about distractors can be found when looking at the percent of test takers responding to each choice. If any of the distractors are selected less than 3% of the time, then this choice is not doing its job, and you might consider replacing it. (Let's hope the options with less than 3% are distractors and not correct answers.)

Sure enough, in our example test, there were six distractors that were never chosen. As you can see, neglected distractors are common. Researchers have indeed shown that instructors find it difficult to write multiple choice items with three tempting distractors (Lord, 1977; Rodriguez, 2005). In two out of the six cases, I would probably keep the distractor as is. In Item 1, the question asks for a "part of the brain," and the choices are one of the four lobes of the brain. There are only four lobes, so it makes sense to include them all. Item 11 asks for a "style of child rearing," and the three choices aside from "all of the above" are actual child-rearing styles cited in *Basic Psychology* by Gleitman (1992) based on research by Baumrind (1967, 1971) and Maccoby & Martin (1983). So, it makes sense to keep these three as well and just change the "all of the above" choice. The other four distractors that were never chosen could be rewritten to become more appealing to students who have not mastered the content. (For curious readers, the other distractors were Choice B of Item 2, Choices A and B of Item 8 (wow - two in one item); and Choice B of Item 9.)

Take note if low-functioning items appear to be of a certain item type, for example, true-false items versus multiple choice items. Then you can make adjustments to the number of each type you are using next time.

In addition to fixing items, you can also look at those that performed well so that you can see what types and features worked. Then you can write more of these in the future.

Summary

This brings us to the conclusion of the UGIFT process. By going through the advised steps, you have successfully:

- **Understood** the score distribution and reliability of your exam

- **Graded** exams making sure to remove any items that functioned poorly

and you have a plan for:

- **Instructing** students based on their exam performance

- **Testing** students in the future with the goal of high reliability, appropriate difficulty, and well-functioning items

Now instead of seeing exam reports as pages of inscrutable numbers, you can appreciate the practical uses of these numbers and apply the underlying information toward improving tests and instruction. And now you have a measurable way to track your own progress over time. You can see (1) if test reliability increases, (2) if exam difficulty matches your planned blueprint more closely, and (3) if the proportion of well-functioning items in your tests increases as well.

Remember to keep things in perspective. Professional test publishers hire professional item writers and reviewers, field test items, run pilots, and conduct studies. You do not have the resources to do these things, so be patient. With time you most certainly will get to where you want to be.

The following chapter delves deeper into specific topics. You have the basics of what you need to tackle exam analysis reports, so feel free to read the rest at your leisure.

CHAPTER 4:

Going Deeper

This chapter explores concepts raised in previous chapters more thoroughly. Most likely you were directed here to get a more detailed answer to a question or more elaboration on a topic.

Means and Averages

Why are there two words in this field (average and mean) with the exact same meaning?

The short answer is that the two words came to the English language independently from two different sources.

Even though the word *average* is more common, the word *mean* is much older. *Mean* came to us from Greek philosophers and astronomers. Aristotle who lived during the 300s BCE, used mean to describe a "point equally distant" from extremes (Aristotle, 1994).

In contrast, the word *average* first appeared in English in the 1700s (Merriam-Webster, n.d.). Its etymology is more mercantile in nature. Basically, the root was borrowed from French (which was itself borrowed from Arabic) and meant the shared expenses from damaged merchandise. The method of dividing the expenses equally among the owners of a damaged ship or cargo was done by computing the mean. Over time, the word *average* gained in popularity and was used in place of the word *mean*. This is why the word *average* is more common today. In math and science contexts, the older term *mean* appears more frequently, especially since there are different kinds of means: arithmetic (the one we are referring to), weighted, geometric, and harmonic.

This information helped to settle my mind. For years, I was concerned that I was missing something important about why one term was used in some places but not others. But at the end of day, the reason was just historical linguistics.

Reliability

Why are there so many terms for alpha?

The equation used most often for estimating test reliability by using one test administration was published in an article written by Lee Cronbach in 1951. In that article, Cronbach set the equation equal to the Greek letter α (alpha), with the intent of labeling it first in reference to other coefficients designated by other Greek letters. (In statistics, a coefficient is a value that tells us the correlation or connection between sets of data. For reliability, we are looking at the relation between scores from two test administrations or between scores from two subtests from the same administration.) Although Cronbach did not invent the coefficient, his seminal paper popularized it, and this is why it is often referred to as Cronbach's coefficient alpha, coefficient alpha, Cronbach's alpha, and alpha.

Because Cronbach did not discover the equation, some in the field have opted to use other terms such as tau-equivalent reliability. This term comes from a description of the data used to derive the equation. The idea is that to compute reliability, you find the correlation of scores from iterations of two subtests that have different items but are parallel, meaning the items have equivalent difficulty. This is a strict assumption that can be relaxed to assume that scores from the two subtests result in theoretical true scores that are either equivalent or are shifted by a constant amount. In the articles by statisticians that discuss these matters, true scores, or scores that are theoretical and tap directly into the knowledge of the person without being muddied by imperfect test items, are often represented as the Greek letter T, pronounced tau. And thus, because the reliability equation is based on test items that result in equivalent true scores (or tau), you have the term tau-equivalent reliability. Most exam-analysis services do not assume that their users are deep into the statistics though and simply use the term alpha.

Why is KR20 called KR20?

The equation that describes how to estimate test reliability when a test has items that are scored as either correct or incorrect (as opposed to partial credit) was published in an article by G. F. Kuder and M. W. Richardson in 1937. The first initials of the authors' last names are KR, and the equation in the paper used most often for estimating reliability is Equation 20.

What is the difference between alpha and KR20?

The two equations are actually mathematically related. (Don't worry – you don't have to know what all of it means. Just notice that they are similar.)

$$\alpha = \frac{n}{n-1}\left(1 - \frac{\sum \sigma_i^2}{\sum \sigma_{test}^2}\right)$$

$$KR_{20} = \frac{n}{n-1}\left(1 - \frac{\sum p_i q_i}{\sum \sigma_{test}^2}\right)$$

The circled sections are the only differences between the two equations. In the alpha equation, σ^2 means variance and the variances across items are summed (Σ). In the KR20 equation, the variances across items are also summed. It is just that the variance for dichotomous data (meaning either correct or incorrect with no partial credit) can be computed in a different way using ps and qs. p is the proportion of people who answered the question correctly and q is $(1 - p)$. So the KR20 equation cannot accommodate situations where a test taker scored 2 out 3 on a short-answer question. Alpha can accommodate such cases. This does not mean that alpha does not handle dichotomous data. Alpha can handle both. If you have dichotomous data and you run it through both the alpha equation and the KR20 equation, you should get the same answer if rounding to hundredths (two decimal places).

Sometimes, instructors assume that you cannot use KR20 for multiple choice tests. You can. Say you have a question with Choices A, B, C, and D, and A is correct. If you mark A as correct and B, C, and D as incorrect, then you have dichotomous data. With dichotomous data you can use either KR20 or alpha (they should give you the same result).

An example of when you cannot us KR20 and must use alpha is when some or all of your questions allow partial credit. Table 13 summarizes when each equation is appropriate.

Table 13. Appropriate Conditions for KR20 vs.
Cronbach's Coefficient Alpha

		How Questions Are Scored	
		Dichotomous (correct, incorrect)	Polytomous (partial credit)
Reliability	KR20	YES	NO
	Cronbach's Coefficient Alpha	YES	YES

How many items do I need for my desired level of reliability?

Many people have asked this question over the years, so statisticians came up with an equation to estimate reliability for different numbers of items on a test. The equation is called the Spearman-Brown prophecy formula. The name credits the two authors who independently published the same equation during the same year (1910).

$$k = \frac{\rho_{desired}\,(1 - \rho_{observed})}{\rho_{observed}\,(1 - \rho_{desired})}$$

where

k is the number of 'tests' (1 would be the length of the current test, 2 would mean twice as many items, and 0.5 would mean half as many items),

$\rho_{observed}$ is the observed reliability you are seeing in the reports,

$\rho_{desired}$ is the reliability you want

Personally, I find the equation to be a bit confusing because it does not give you the number of items but rather the proportion of the number of items in the current test. To compute the total number of items needed, just multiply k by the number of items in your current test. We have also created a calculator that you can use on our website:

www.intelliphonics.com $\rightarrow$ Resources $\rightarrow$ Number of Items

Standard Error of Measurement (SEM)

Why is .68 in the following explanation?
> If Maria scored an 88, then the likelihood that her true score is 88 +/-3 (somewhere between 85 and 91 points) is .68.

The likelihood of .68 comes from the normal distribution. In the normal distribution, the area under the entire curve is 1. You can also compute the area of different sections. So the area under the curve between one standard deviation below the mean and one standard deviation above the mean is .68 as shown in Figure 12.

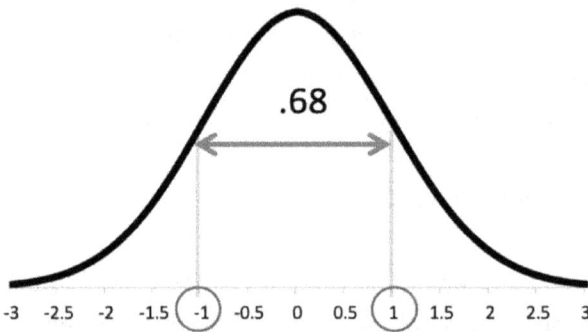

Figure 12. The area under the curve of a normal distribution between one standard deviation below and above the mean is .68.

How do we know it is .68? We know the formula for the normal distribution thanks to Carl Friedrich Gauss, and we also know calculus thanks to Isaac Newton and Gottfried Leibniz. With this knowledge, we can compute the area under the curve. By knowing the area, we also know that if we were to pick one point from the distribution at random, then the likelihood of picking a point between -1 and 1 standard deviations would be .68. So what does this have to do with Maria's score?

Imagine that instead of taking just one test, Maria took thousands of tests, and each test score was a point in a frequency distribution. Given what we know about nature, the shape of the distribution of test scores would actually resemble the normal distribution. Let's say her true score was 86 with a standard error of measurement of 3. (The true score reflects what she really knows.) With an observed score of 88, her true score of 86 is indeed in the range of 88 +/-3 (85 to 91).

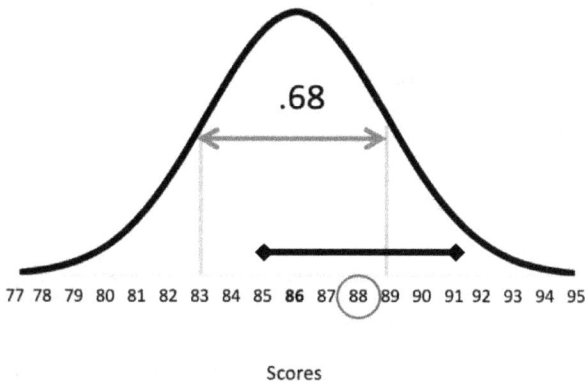

.68

77 78 79 80 81 82 83 84 85 **86** 87 88 89 90 91 92 93 94 95

Scores

Figure 13. Distribution of theoretical observed scores when the true score is 86 and the standard error of measurement is 3.

If, however, the observed score were 79, then no, her true score would be out of range since 86 is not between 79 +/-3 (76 to 82). Basically, if the observed score is 83,

84, 85, 86, 87, 88 or 89, then the true score of 86 will appear in the range of the observed score +/-3. Given what we know about the normal distribution, the likelihood that the observed scores of 83, 84, 85, 86, 87, 88, and 89 would be pulled at random from the thousands of Maria's test scores is .68. Ok, you might say, that's all fine and good if her true score is 86, but what if it's not. What if her true score is 80?

If her true score is 80, then the distribution would have 80 as the mean. The curve would just be shifted with the same shape. Then the range of 88 +/-3 would not contain the true score because 88 would be in the tail on the right side of the distribution. The likelihood of the true score NOT being in the observed score range is .32. This will happen when the observed score is too far in one of the tails. Unfortunately, you can never know because you can only guess at the true score.

Now you can increase the likelihood that the true score will appear in the range, but if you do this, you have to increase the range. For 95% confidence that the true score is in the range, the range becomes the observed score +/- 1.96 SEM (because when the area under the curve is .95, the section is 1.96 standard deviations above and below the mean). If you round this up to two times the SEM, then the range would be 88 +/-6 (82 to 94).

What is the equation that shows that SEM is related to reliability?

$$SEM = s\sqrt{1-r}$$

where

s is the standard deviation, and

r is the reliability of the test.

You may also come across a similar equation:

$$SEM = \sigma\sqrt{1-\rho}$$

where

σ is the standard deviation, and

ρ is the reliability of the test.

The difference between the two is the top equation uses symbols for a sample and the bottom uses symbols for a population. Often is statistics you make inferences about a population based on a sample of people and the equations you use for samples and populations are slightly different because of bias when estimating standard deviations. You don't have to worry about these issues because you are simply looking at reports instead of building the system yourself. Folks who actually build these systems spend time thinking about these issues so that you have the best tools available to you for understanding your exams and we kindly thank them for it.

Cumulative Percent

Why does my report not include the current score when reporting the cumulative percent?

One reason cumulative percent may not include the current score is because cumulative frequency/percent is often used as a step in the process of computing percentile rank, and the creators of the report want to be responsible in how they deal with frequencies of the current score when they present the percentile rank. Imagine that the score of 55 is actually somewhere in the interval between 54.5 and 55.4. Some academics want to assume that scores of 55 are evenly distributed across the interval; namely, not all of them are pegged at the top at 55.4. If you assume that they are all at the top, then they would all be included in percentile rank. But because many assume that the scores are distributed, official equations for percentile rank use only half of the frequency value of the current score (because it is assumed that half of the scores of 55 are in the range of 54.5 and 54.9 and the other half are in the range of 55.0 and 55.4. So, as part of the equation, you use the cumulative frequency of all the scores lower than the current score in one of the steps.

Z-Scores

How do you use z-scores for score interpretation?

On some Score Distribution reports, scores are sometimes transposed into values called z-scores, which are commonly used to describe the normal distribution. In a normal distribution, the mean is 0 and z-scores describe how many standard deviations a point is above or below the mean. For example, a z-score of 1.00 tells you that the score is one standard deviation above the mean and a z-score of negative 1.00 tells you the score is one standard deviation below the mean. If the distribution of your test scores resembles the normal distribution, then you can get a sense for the percent of students within different ranges of z-scores. For example, 68% of students will scores between the z-scores of -1.00 and 1.00 (if the distribution is normal).

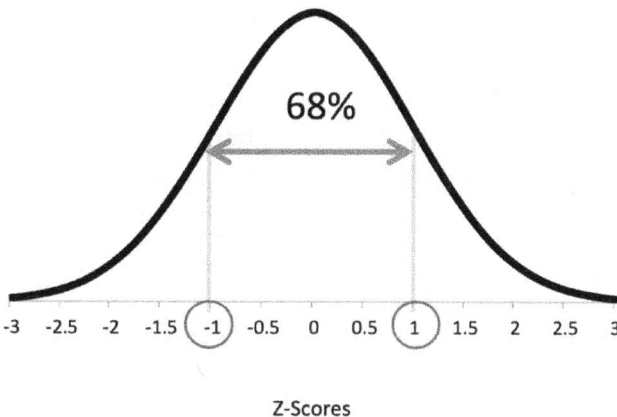

68%

-3 -2.5 -2 -1.5 -1 -0.5 0 0.5 1 1.5 2 2.5 3

Z-Scores

Figure 14. Z-scores from a normal distribution.

This information is useful for comparing performance on different exams that have a different number of total possible points. Now you have a standard scale for comparison. If, for example, the z-scores for a student across multiple tests are consistently below -1.00, then this student may need some intervention. Some teachers also use this information for grading purposes (page 73, Grading on a Bell Curve).

How do you compute a z-score?

$$z\text{-}score = \frac{test\ score - mean}{standard\ deviation}$$

Here is an example.
mean: 6.48
standard deviation: 2.08
test score: 9

$$z\text{-}score = \frac{9 - 6.48}{2.08} = 1.21$$

If you are using a spreadsheet, then equations can be written in cells to do the computation for you. If a test score is in cell A1, you might write the following formula in cell B1, for example:

=(A1-6.48)/2.08

Appendix A

Test questions and answer choices for an example psychology test. The boldfaced choice was intended to be the correct answer.

1   Visual images from the eye are sent to which part of the brain?
    A. frontal lobe
    B. occipital lobe
    C. parietal lobe
    D. temporal lobe

2   Cognitive Theorist is to Behaviorist as _____ is to _____
    A. knowledge / action
    B. conditioning / extinction
    C. stimulus / response
    D. Pavlov / Skinner

3   Which is an example of a top-down process?
    A. seeing basic features of a letter such as a horizontal line
    B. expecting what the last word in a sentence will be
    C. separating sounds into individual words
    D. detecting a grammatical error in written text

4   Which is NOT an effect in common
      theories of memory?
      A. episodic effect
      B. primacy effect
      C. recency effect
      D. none of the above

5   Why are human estimates of likelihood
      often incorrect?
      A. People misinterpret expected values.
      B. People resist stereotypes.
      C. People create faulty frequency
          distributions.
      D. People ignore the base rate.

6   What is a common phenomenon observed
      in language acquisition?
      **A. Children overgeneralize -ed for past
          tense.**
      B. Children respond with "no."
      C. Mothers correct grammatical errors.
      D. Children confuse possessives with
          appositives.

7   With the self-serving bias, people tend to
      do what?
      A. deny the existence of a failure
      B. view a neutral situation as a success
      **C. claim that an outside force caused a
          failure**
      D. share credit for a success with other
          people

8   What is one reason for conformity?
     A. diffusing responsibility for bystander
         apathy
     B. understanding that thorough research
         cannot be conducted in time
     C. believing that one can lead the group
         in the right direction
     D. wanting to be liked

9   A toy is hidden from a child and the child
     doesn't look for it. According to Piaget,
     why is this?
     A. failure of conservation
     B. proactive habituation
     C. no concept of object permanence
     D. perceptual effect of occlusion

10   Studies with identical twins and fraternal
     twins have shown what?
     A. personality inventories are valid
     B. temperament is more stable with
         identical twins
     C. coping patterns are subject to social
         learning
     **D. heredity accounts for some
         personality traits**

11   Which is a style of child rearing?

    A. autocratic

    B. permissive

    C. authoritative-reciprocal

    D. all of the above

12   What is the canonical threshold for statistical significance?

    A. $p < .025$

    B. $p < .05$

    C. $p < .15$

    D. $p < .95$

References

American Educational Research Association (AERA), American Psychological Association (APA), National Council on Measurement in Education (NCME). (2014). *Standards for educational and psychological testing.* Washington, DC: American Educational Research Association.

Aristotle. (1994). *Nichomachean ethics.* Cambridge, MA: Harvard University Press.

Baumrind, D. (1967). Child care practices anteceding three patterns of preschool behavior. *Genetic Psychology Monographs, 75,* 43-88.

Baumrind, D. (1971). Current patterns of parental authority. *Genetic Psychology Monographs 1.*

Brown, W. (1910). Some experimental results in the correlation of mental abilities. *British Journal of Psychology, 3,* 296-322.

Cronbach, L.J. (1951). Coefficient alpha and the internal structure of tests. *Psychometrika, 16,* 297-334.

Ebel, R.L. (1954). Procedures for the analysis of classroom tests, *Educational and Psychological Measurement, 14,* 352-364.

Gleitman, H. (1992). *Basic psychology.* WW Norton & Company.

Kahneman, D., & Tversky, A. (1973). On the psychology of prediction. *Psychology Review, 80*(4), 237-251.

Kelley, T.L. (1939). Selection of upper and lower groups for the validation of test items. *Journal of Educational Psychology, 30,* 17-24.

Kuder, G.F. & Richardson, M.W. (1937). The theory of the estimation of test reliability. *Psychometrika, 2*(3), 151-160.

Lord, F.M. (1952). The relationship of reliability of multiple-choice test to the distribution of item difficulties. *Psychometrika, 18,* 181-194.

Lord, F. M. (1977). Optimal number of choices per item—A comparison of four approaches. *Journal of Educational Measurement, 14*(1), 33-38.

Maccoby, E.E., & Martin, J.A. (1983). Socialization in the context of the family: Parent-child interaction. In P.H. Mussen (Ed.), *Carmichael's manual of child psychology: Vol. 4. Socialization, personality and social development* (M.E. Hetherington, volume editor) (pp. 1-120). Wiley.

Merriam-Webster. (n.d.). Average. In Merriam-Webster.com dictionary. Retrieved from https://www.merriam-webster.com/dictionary/average

Mertler, C.A. (2003). *Classroom assessment: A practical guide for educators.* Los Angeles, CA: Pyrczak.

Mueller, D.J (1975). An assessment of the effectiveness of complex alternatives in multiple choice achievement test items. *Educational and Psychological Measurement, 35,* 135-141.

Poundstone, W. (2014). *Rock breaks scissors: A practical guide to outguessing and outwitting almost everybody.* New York: Little, Brown and Company.

Rodriguez, M. C. (2005). Three options are optimal for multiple-choice items: A meta-analysis of 80 years of research. *Educational Measurement: Issues and Practice, 24*(2), 3-13.

Sindelar, N.W. (2003). Using data to increase student achievement, step-by-step. Classroom Leadership, 6(6). Retrieved from http://www.ascd.org/publications/classroom_leadership/mar2003/Using_Data_to_Increase_Student_Achievement,_Step-by-Step.aspx

Spearman, C.C. (1910). Correlation calculated from faulty data. *British Journal of Psychology, 3,* 271-295.

University of Wisconsin, Oshkosh. (2020). Optimal item difficulty. Retrieved from uwosh.edu/testing/faculty-information/test-scoring/score-report-interpretation/item-analysis-1/item-difficulty

Vegada, B. N., Karelia, B. N., & Philai, A. (2014). Reliability of four-response type multiple choice questions of pharmacology summative tests of II M.B.B.S. students. *International Journal of Mathematics and Statistics Invention, 2*(1), 6-10.

Index